James Monroe

# The company drill of the infantry of the line

With the skirmishing drill of the company and battalion, after the method of Gen.

Le Louterel.

James Monroe

**The company drill of the infantry of the line**
*With the skirmishing drill of the company and battalion, after the method of Gen. Le Louterel.*

ISBN/EAN: 9783741175855

Manufactured in Europe, USA, Canada, Australia, Japa

Cover: Foto ©Andreas Hilbeck / pixelio.de

Manufactured and distributed by brebook publishing software (www.brebook.com)

James Monroe

**The company drill of the infantry of the line**

THE

# COMPANY DRILL

OF THE

# INFANTRY OF THE LINE,

TOGETHER WITH THE

## SKIRMISHING DRILL

OF THE

## COMPANY AND BATTALION,

AFTER THE METHOD OF GEN. LE LOUTEREL.

## BAYONET FENCING.

With a Supplement on the Handling and Service of Light Infantry.

BY

## J. MONROE,

COL. 22D REGIMENT, N. Y. S. MILITIA; FORMERLY CAPTAIN
UNITED STATES INFANTRY.

NEW YORK:
D. VAN NOSTRAND, 192 BROADWAY.
1863.

Entered, according to Act of Congress, in the year 1862, by

D. VAN NOSTRAND,

In the Clerk's Office of the District Court of the United States for the Southern District of New York.

# PREFACE.

MORE than a year ago the author of this small volume, executed the translation of about one-fourth of the Battalion Exercise of General De Louterel, but avocations both civil and military interrupted the work, and in the mean time Lippincott, of Philadelphia, brought out the translation of the drill of the Battalion and the Evolutions of the Line, by Captain Coppée. But the Company Drill has not till now been offered to the public. I have modified the original so far as to conform to the existing system. The method of Le Louterel must have been well received in France. I have taken the *seventh* edition of his work.

An examination of the volume will best explain the peculiarities that distinguish it. Le Louterel did not apply his system to the skirmishing drill, further than the deployment and rally of the *battalion*. It will be found applied in this volume to the *whole* of the skirmishing drill. In addition to the introduction of the doubling and undoubling of files (not found in the original), I have systematically compared the movements with the French *Ordonnance* of 1861.

The Bayonet Fencing is taken from the same *Ordonnance*. It is remarkable for its simplicity and the great facility of its acquisition, and it carries the approval of the highest authority of France.

In the supplement will be found some suggestions that will perhaps be acceptable to the intelligent classes who now fill the army, and who, however unused formerly to military ideas, adopt the leading principle of aiming to improve whatever they engage in.

Some allowance for trifling errors may be needed, in consequence of the fact that the volume comes out during the absence of the author in the field.

|   | PAGE. |
|---|---|
| General principles of fencing | 11 |
| Fencing with the bayonet | 14 |
| Shortenings | 26 |
| Lessons for practice | 29 |
| School of the company | 31 |
| To open ranks | 32 |
| Alignments in open ranks | 33 |
| Manual of arms (in open ranks) | 34 |
| To close ranks | 35 |
| Alignments and manual in closed ranks | 35 |
| Loading in four times and at will | 36 |
| The fire by company | 37 |
| The fire by file | 38 |
| The fire by rank | 39 |
| The fire by the rear rank | 39 |
| To advance in line of battle | 42 |
| To halt and align the company | 43 |
| Oblique march in line of battle | 44 |
| The march in retreat | 45 |
| The march by the flank | 48 |
| To change direction by file | 50 |
| To halt the company and face it to the front | 50 |
| Doubling and undoubling files | 51 |

## CONTENTS.

| | PAGE. |
|---|---|
| To form the company on the right or left by file into line | 53 |
| The company marching by the flank to form company or platoon, and to face them in marching | 57 |
| To break into column by platoon | 61 |
| To march into column | 65 |
| To change direction | 66 |
| To halt the column | 69 |
| Being in column, to form to the right or left into line | 70 |
| To break into platoons and to re-form the company | 73 |
| To break files to the rear, and to bring them again into line | 77 |
| The march in column of route | 80 |
| Countermarch | 86 |
| To form column by platoon on the right or left into line | 88 |
| Formation of the company from one rank into two ranks, and reciprocally, and from two ranks into four, and reciprocally | 92 |
| The company in two ranks being in march by the front, and right in front | 96 |
| Deployments | 99 |
| To deploy forward | 99 |
| To deploy by the flank | 105 |
| To extend and to close intervals | 109 |
| To close intervals | 112 |
| To support and to relieve skirmishers | 114 |
| The movement of deployed lines | 116 |
| To advance the line | 116 |

## CONTENTS.

> firings.............................................
fire marching to the front....................
fire marching in retreat.....................
fire marching by the flank...................
> rallies............................................
rally by sections.............................
ly by platoons...............................
ly on the reserve............................
rmishers in square and column................
> assembly.........................................
semble on the reserve.........................
nœuvres of skirmishers........................
ployment of skirmishers from column..........
lies.............................................
>plement..........................................
lies.............................................
nk deployments, &c............................
anges of front................................

## GENERAL PRINCIPLES OF FENCING.

Fencing is the opposition of force with the edge or point of weapons held in the hand, and resembles both boxing with the closed hand and hurling a missile. It depends upon the correct attitude and movements of the body, and the lines of direction of the instrument, or weapon, employed.

The body resting erect upon the feet brought together, is supported upon a base that is narrow and consequently weak—a slight pressure, in that case, will overset it, and the higher the point of such pressure, the less the overturning force required; but when one foot is advanced, the side turned, and the rearward line of the body slanted, as nature herself instructs, when a weight is to be heaved, or an obstacle pushed, or resisted, the position is many times stronger. The base of support has been broadened, the height of the figure lessened, and the relations of mutual support so established as to apply the true leverage of the whole framework.

The body so propped and poised, the weapon (say, a sword) is to be advanced in such a manner

fencer and menace his adversary. This, referri[ng]
to both the man and sword, constitutes the po[si]
tion of *guard*.

*Guard*, then, is a position in which to defend [an]
attack.

*Parry* is a movement made from *guard*, with t[he]
weapon, to meet and ward off an adversary's [at]
tack.

*Thrust* (lunge) or *cut* is a directing of the poi[nt]
or edge, against the adversary.

From every *parry* a thrust may be delivered[;]
this is called *counter-thrusting*.

From every thrust or parry, you may return [di]
rectly to the position of *guard*.

There are two general relations of the weap[on]
from which all the rest are derived. These a[re]
*carte* and *tierce*. Carte guard and carte parries a[re]
inside; and tierce are outside. That is, carte [is]
on the side of the breast, and tierce on the side [of]
the back. For example, with the sword, where [it]
is the right foot and side that are advanced, car[te]
is the guard, or the parades, made toward the fe[n]
cer's left, meant to cover attacks on that si[de.]
Tierce, in all respects, the opposite. But with t[he]
bayonet, the case is reversed, because then it [is]
the left side and foot that are in advance. He[nce]
therefore, the carte side of the weapon is that [to]
its right, and tierce is outward or left.

*Feint*.—To menace an attack in one directio[n]
and deliver it in another. It is, as the word i[m]
ports, a movement intended to deceive the adv[er]
sary, or to throw him off his guard.

*Timing* is anticipating an adversary by proje[cting]

## GENERAL PRINCIPLES.

preparing himself to thrust. None but an expert fencer can execute effectively the time thrust.

The simple and direct thrusts are the best. Complex combinations are good for exercise and practice, as they confer facility of action.

*Opposition*, is the outward bearing of the weapon when a thrust is delivered, intended to bear the adverse point out of line. It must always be preserved, otherwise there is danger of an *interchanged* thrust.

In thrusting, let the *point* reach its limit at the moment the *body* is thrown forward to *its* extent. Let the whole act be simultaneous.

It is never safe to take the point off the body of a skilful antagonist. It should be constantly kept interposed, even in the parries. (In the instances of using the butt of the piece, the guard is supposed to be broken up, and then the butt itself stands in lieu of point.)

The point, in *guard*, should be so far raised as that the upper parries, inside and out, may cover the *body*, from the head to the legs. A thrust cannot be made, with the bayonet, at the lower limbs, without fatally exposing the thruster. Hence parries below are unnecessary and inartful, because in making such parries, the return thrusts from them would be the adoption and imitation of that which is itself a fault. The French system has wisely discarded all the low parries and thrusts.

All hanging guards, wherein the position of the piece when on guard (*point* higher than *hilt*) is reversed, that is, positions that throw up the butt and drop the point, are weak and unreliable.

The weapon may, in its length, be divided into three equal parts. The first third is that nearest to the holder; this is the *forte*, or strong part of the weapon; the second part is the *medium* or middle, and the *last* is the *faible* or weak part. The *leverage* or universal principle of all fencing is, by movements and flexures of the body and limbs, and by collisions of the pieces to bring one's *forte* into contest with the *faible* of the adversary. When art does this, mere strength cannot reply to it.

The short treatise which follows is taken entire from the French system of 1861. It is much simplified, and having been revised by their ▇rd of officers, as stated in the Emperor's decree; it may be regarded as the result and selection out of the numerous methods proposed of late years, in France. Its distinguishing features are: 1st. Natural and simple methods of movement. 2d. The employment of upward guards and parries only. 3d. The discarding of the *development*, as unsuited to a two-handed and weighty weapon—such as the musket and bayonet—which is a true *pike*.

## FENCING WITH THE BAYONET.

The men are formed in one rank with intervals of four paces between them, in order that they may not interfere with one another when they are executing the *volts*.

The pieces are carried at the right shoulder, that

BAYONET FENCING. 15

is, in the "Light Infantry," or sergeant's manner of carrying the small arm.*

The soldier, or the squad, being at shouldered arms, the instructor commands:

1. *Guard against infantry.* 2. GUARD.

---

* Piece in right hand—barrel nearly vertical, and resting in hollow of shoulder—guard to the front, right arm extended nearly to its full length, thumb and fore-finger embracing the guard—the other fingers closed on the handle of the piece—little-finger supporting the dog (the plate along the right thigh)—the left hand by the left side.

## One time and two motions.

FIRST MOTION.—Make a half-face to the right in turning on the heels, bringing the left toe to the front and the right toe to the right, the feet square to each other; raise at the same time, the piece slightly, and seize it with the left hand above and near the lower band.

SECOND MOTION.—Carry the right foot twenty inches to the rear, its heel on a perpendicular line with the left heel, the feet at right angles, the knees slightly bent, the weight of the body borne equally by the two legs; bring down the piece with both hands, the barrel upward, the left elbow against the body; seize the piece at the same time below the guard (*i. e.* at the handle), with the right hand, the arms falling naturally, the bayonet slightly elevated. (The left arm is consequently a little bent.)

### SHOULDER ARMS.

Raise the piece with the left hand, place it against the right shoulder, and at the same time, bring up the right heel on the alignment of the left, in facing to the front.

1. *Guard against cavalry.* 2. GUARD.

The same as "guard against infantry," except that the right hand rests at the hip, and the bayonet is at the height of the eye, as in the movement of "charge bayonet."

The men placed in either of the foregoing posi-

BAYONET FENCING. 17

tions of "guard," will execute the following movements:

1. *Right (or left).*  2. FACE.

Turn on the left heel, raising the toe, and face to the right (or left), at the same time carry around the right foot one quarter of the circle, and twenty inches in rear of the left.

1. *Right about.*  2. FACE.

Turn about to the rear, by the right on the left

heel, raising the left toe, without altering the position of the piece, and carry the right foot around to the rear, twenty inches from the left.

1. *Left about.* 2. FACE.

Turn on the left heel, to the left, the reverse of the last movement above.

1. *Step to the front.* 2. MARCH.

Bring up the right foot behind the left, and carry the left twenty inches in advance of the right (keeping the knee bent during the movement).

1. *Step to the rear.* 2. MARCH.

Draw back the left foot against the right, and plant the right to the rear twenty inches.

1. *Step to the right.* 2. MARCH.

Throw the right foot twenty inches to the right, and in the same direction, immediately carry the left foot in front of it, at its proper distance and position.

1. *Step to the left.* 2. MARCH.

Throw the left foot twenty inches to the left, and promptly place the right foot at its proper distance in rear.

## BAYONET FENCING. 19

1. *Double step to the front.* 2. MARCH.

Throw the right foot twenty inches in front of the left, and briskly plant the left, twenty inches in advance of the right, preserving the position of "guard."

1. *Double step to the rear.* 2. MARCH.

Throw the left foot fourteen inches to the rear of the right (passing it on its left), and carry the right twenty inches in rear of the left, preserving the position of "guard."

1. *Volt to the right.* 2. MARCH.

Bring up the left arm and hand, the barrel opposite the left shoulder, without moving the right hand. Turn to the right on the right toe, throw the left foot perpendicularly to the rear twenty inches, finishing the volt on the left toe, and bringing the right foot to its position in rear, at the same time bring the piece to the position of "guard."

1. *Volt to the left.* 2. MARCH.

Turn to the left on the right toe, carry the left foot perpendicularly to the rear twenty inches, and finish the volt in a way the reverse of the above.

When the men are well established in these various positions, and can execute the several steps and volts with ease and precision, they will be taught the attack and defence with the bayonet.

### 1. *In carte.* 2. Parry.

At the second command, lift the muzzle a full foot (thirteen inches) with the left hand, without moving the right, at the same time make a parry to the right of about six inches, and remain in that position.

### Guard.

Lower promptly the left hand without moving the right, and bring back the piece to the position of " guard."

Whenever the instructor causes the parries and thrusts to be executed, he will at the end of each movement command " guard," at which the men will resume that position.

### 1. *In tierce.* 2. Parry.

Raise promptly the piece one foot with the left hand, without moving the right, at the same time making a parry with the piece to the left, about six inches.

### 1. *In prime.* 2. Parry.

Spring up the piece to cover the head, holding it with both hands and the arms fully extended, the lockplate turned toward the body, the bayonet slightly inclined to the left, the lower band at the height of the top of the cap (the piece is

BAYONET FENCING. 21

nearly horizontal, butt to the rear, point to the front, hands held vertical).

1. *In prime to the right.* 2. PARRY.

Advance the left shoulder and parry prime toward the right.

1. *In prime to the left.* 2. PARRY.

Advance the right shoulder, and parry in prime to the left.

The last two parries are to oppose attacks from above—as from cavalry or a breast-work.

The prime parry is intended as a general protection for the head; the piece is moved around in the two hands as if on a pivot.—*Translator*.

1. *In carte.* 2. THRUST.

From the position of "guard," throw forward the weight of the body, bend the left knee and

BAYONET FENCING. 23

straighten the right, project the left arm to its full extent, the fingers of the left hand opened and sustaining the piece, the butt in front of the nipple of the right breast, and the lockplate underneath.

Remain in this position until the command "guard."

Turning the lockplate underneath, gives the piece in the thrust a rotatory action.—*Translator.*

1. *In tierce.*   2. THRUST.

24            BAYONET FENCING.

Throw forward the upper part of the body, straighten the right leg, and bend the left knee, extend the left arm to its full length, the fingers opened, and sustaining the piece, turn the guard, lockplate upward, guard to the right, the butt in front of the right breast (its nipple).

1. *In prime.*   2. THRUST.

Raise the piece with both hands, the arms ex-

tended above the head, the guard upward, the barrel between the fingers of the left hand, bend the left knee, and straighten the right, at the same time direct the point in thrusting at the height of an adversary on horseback.

1. *In prime to the right (or left)*.  2. THRUST.

Advance the left shoulder, and thrust to the right (or the right shoulder, and thrust to the left).

The thrust of prime has three general directions—direct to the front, to the right, and to the left—answering to the prime parried.—*Translator*.

### Longe.

Throw forward the upper part of the body, bending the left leg, and straightening the right, push rapidly the point toward the adversary the whole length of the right arm, abandoning it for the moment with the left, and come back to guard (without any command).

When on guard, as "against infantry," the blow (in thrusting) will be directed at the height of the breast.

In the guard against cavalry, the point will be directed at the height of a horse's head, or a horseman's side.

### Shortenings.

The *shortenings* of the guard are necessary in a *mêlée*, or in foiling an attempt to break within the guard. They should be as simple, natural, and rapidly formed as possible, and permit an instant return to the guard.

1. *In carte.*  2. SHORTEN.

From either guard (against infantry or cavalry), throw back the piece to the full extension of the right arm, slipping the left hand up at the same time, to the bayonet clasp, left hand at the centre of the breast.

# BAYONET FENCING.

GUARD.

Throw forward the piece, to the position of guard, bringing back the left hand.

1. *In tierce.*  2. SHORTEN.

Throw the piece upward, and backward to the extend of the right arm, turning the barrel underneath, slipping the left hand to the bayonet clasp, the hand at the centre of the upper part of the breast, the piece nearly horizontal.

28                BAYONET FENCING.

GUARD.

Lower rapidly the piece to guard, turning the barrel upward, and replacing the left hand.

After the men have perfectly learned the various steps, parries, and thrusts, they will be taught to combine them, as follows:

1. *Double step to the front, in prime parry, and thrust.* 2. MARCH.

At the word of execution—MARCH—the soldier

will execute the *double step*, will *parry*, and will *thrust in prime*.

As a soldier may be compelled to defend himself against two or three men at once, he will be made to execute double movements, and double thrusts, which will considerably increase his skill and activity, for example:

1. *One pace to the front—Longe—Volt to the left—In carte parry and thrust.*  2. MARCH.

At the command MARCH, *step to the front, longe* (take the position of guard), *execute the volt to the left, parry in carte* and *thrust carte*.

### Lessons for Practice.

#### I.

1. *In carte* PARRY—*In carte* THRUST.
2. *In tierce* PARRY—*In tierce* THRUST.
3. *In carte* THRUST—*In carte* PARRY.
4. *In tierce* THRUST—*In tierce* PARRY.
5. *In prime* PARRY—*In prime* THRUST.
6. *In prime* THRUST—*In prime* PARRY.
7. GUARD AGAINST INFANTRY—GUARD AGAINST CAVALRY.
8. GUARD AGAINST CAVALRY—GUARD AGAINST INFANTRY.

#### II.

1. *In carte* PARRY—*In tierce* PARRY.
2. *In tierce* PARRY—*In carte* PARRY.
3. *In carte* PARRY—*In prime* PARRY.
4. *In tierce* PARRY—*In prime* PARRY.
5. *In prime* PARRY—*In carte* PARRY.
6. *In prime* PARRY—*In tierce* PARRY.

7. *In carte, in tierce, in prime* PARRY.
8. *In tierce, in carte, in prime* PARRY.
9. *In prime, in carte, in tierce* PARRY.
10. *In prime, in tierce, in carte* PARRY.

### III.

1. *In carte* THRUST, *in prime* PARRY, *in prime* THRUST.
2. *In prime* PARRY, *in prime to the left* THRUST, *in carte* PARRY, *in carte* THRUST.
3. *In tierce* THRUST, *in prime* PARRY, *in prime to the left* THRUST, *in tierce* PARRY.
4. *In carte—tierce—prime,* PARRY, *in prime* THRUST.
5. *In tierce—carte—prime* PARRY, *in prime* THRUST.
6. *In prime—carte, and tierce* PARRY, *in tierce* THRUST.
7. *In prime—tierce—carte* PARRY, *in carte* THRUST.

The foregoing movements originate from the position of *guard*, and when finished, the soldier at once returns to *guard*, without any order.

The movements may be combined with the steps, the volts and the facings.

The chief point required is facility in handling the piece correctly in the various oppositions and attacks. The attainment of this divides itself into two parts: 1st, the readiness to throw the piece and person into the several individual positions, and 2d, the rapid transition from one position to another.

The nicety of the sword exercise is inapplicable to the bayonet—the principles that govern the two are the same—but the applications vary widely. The dispute with the bayonet is necessarily brief, and its whole handling ought to be *simple* and *direct.*

# SCHOOL OF THE COMPANY.

THE first sergeant commands, *Fall in*, repeated by the other sergeants. The corporals and privates form in two ranks in the order of height from right to left—the tallest corporal on the right and the shortest on the left of the front rank—distance between the ranks thirteen inches—the pieces at *order arms.*

The first sergeant then places himself four paces in front of the centre, facing to the company, and calls the roll. This finished, he faces about, and reports the result to the officer commanding the company, who at a position four paces in rear of the sergeant, has superintended the roll-call. The sergeant next takes post on the right of the front rank, when the captain marks off the platoons and sections, and places the taller of the remaining two corporals on the left of the first platoon, and the other corporal on the right of the second, both in the front rank. The first platoon must have an *even number* of files. The captain then commands, *In each rank—count twos—*when the two men of the first file call out *one*, those of the next file *two*, the third file *one*, the fourth file *two*, and so on to the left. The files thus numbered, the file-closers take their posts, two paces in rear of the rear rank.

| Explanations. | Commands | |
|---|---|---|
| | of Instructor. | of Capt. or Lt. |

## FIRST LESSON.

### To open ranks.

| | | |
|---|---|---|
| The company being at ordered arms, the instructor directs the left guide to place himself on the left of the front rank, and then commands............ | 1. *Attention.*<br>2. *Company.*<br>3. *Shoulder arms.*<br>4. *To the rear open order.* | |
| The right and left guides step to rear the distance of four paces (of 28 inches). The instructor, at the right flank, sees that they mark correctly the alignment for the rear rank................ | 5. *March.* | |
| The rear rank steps to the rear, and is aligned between the two guides by the first sergeant............... | 6. *Front.* | |
| The left guide takes | | |

# ALIGNMENTS IN OPEN RANKS. 33

| Explanations. | Commands | |
|---|---|---|
| | of Instructor. | of Capt. or Lt. |
| his post as a file-closer, and the rank of file-closers place themselves two paces from the rear rank. | | |

## Alignments in open ranks.

| | | |
|---|---|---|
| Having marched two, or four, men on the right or the left of each rank two or three paces forward, the instructor commands.......... | *By file (right or left)*—Dress. | |
| The men of each rank move upon the line successively, preceded by their neighbor on the side of the alignment two paces, align themselves on the basis, and cast eyes to the front without a command. | | |
| After the successive alignments, the ranks are aligned entire (on a basis as above) forward, backward, and on a line parallel or oblique to the original one. The in- | | |

| EXPLANATIONS. | COMMANDS | |
|---|---|---|
| | OF INSTRUCTOR. | OF CAPT. OR LT. |
| ·structor commands.... | 1. *Right* (or *left*)—DRESS. <br> 2. FRONT. <br> OR <br> 1. *Right* (or *left*) *backward*, DRESS. <br> 2. FRONT. | |

When the alignment is oblique, in *opened* ranks, the rear rank men need not cover their file leaders.

It all the alignments, the captain and covering sergeant are on the flank of the side of alignment—each superintends his rank, and when these are *open*, passes, after each aligning, along its front, to make corrections.

### Manual of arms (in open ranks).

The instructor, placed on the flank so as to see both ranks, commands the manual in the following order:

| | |
|---|---|
| *Present arms.* | *Shoulder arms.* |
| *Order arms.* | |
| *Ground arms.* | |
| *Raise arms.* | *Shoulder arms.* |
| *Support arms.* | *Shoulder arms.* |
| *Fix bayonet.* | *Shoulder arms.* |
| *Charge bayonet.* | *Shoulder arms.* |
| *Trail arms.* | *Shoulder arms.* |
| *Unfix bayonet.* | *Shoulder arms.* |
| *Secure arms.* | *Shoulder arms* |
| *Load in nine times.* | |

ALIGNMENTS AND MANUAL IN CLOSED RANKS. 35

| EXPLANATIONS. | COMMANDS | |
|---|---|---|
| | OF INSTRUCTOR. | OF CAPT. OR LT. |

### To close ranks.

| | | |
|---|---|---|
| The rear rank closes on the front, each man directing himself on his file leader. | 1. *Close order.* 2. MARCH. | |
| Ranks are always opened and closed in *quick* time. | | |

### Alignments and manual in closed ranks.

| | | |
|---|---|---|
| Every thing is executed as in opened ranks, except that the captain, not the instructor, commands... | ............ | 2. FRONT. |
| and except that, in the manual, *Ground arms*, *Raise arms*, and *Secure arms*, are omitted. | | |
| If the instructor wishes to rest the men, still preserving the alignment, at an order, or support, he commands | *In place.* REST. | |
| The men will keep one or other heel on the alignment. | | |

| EXPLANATIONS. | COMMANDS | |
|---|---|---|
| | OF INSTRUCTOR. | OF CAPT. OR LT. |
| But if he wish to rest without keeping the dress.............. | REST. | |
| And the men merely do not quit their ranks. After the latter rest (but not after the former), the ranks are to be dressed anew, whenever the command is given.............. | 1. *Attention.* 2. *Company.* 3. *Shoulder—* ARMS. | |

As a more complete rest, the instructor may, at ordered arms, command *Stack arms*, and, 1. *Break ranks.* 2. MARCH, afterward re-forming the company by the commands, *Fall in*, and *Take arms*.

### SECOND LESSON.

#### Loading in four times and at will.

These two loadings are executed as in the School of the Soldier. In both of them the captain and covering sergeant half face to the right with the men at *prime*, and face to the front when the company (or the man on their left) *shoulders*.

## THE FIRE BY COMPANY.

| Explanations. | Commands | |
|---|---|---|
| | Of Instructor. | Of Capt. or Lt. |

### The fire by company.

| | | |
|---|---|---|
| The instructor......  | 1. *Fire by company.* | |
| The covering sergeant falls back into the line of file-closers, and the captain places himself four paces in rear of that line opposite the centre of the company............ | 2. *Commence firing.* | |
| The captain adds... | ............ | 1. *Company,* <br> 2. Ready. <br> 3. Aim. <br> 4. Fire. <br> 5. Load. |
| The pieces being reloaded and at a ready, the captain repeats the last three commands till the *roll*. | | |
| To stop the firing... | *Cease firing.* | *Cease firing.* |
| To recall the captain and sergeant into line.. | Posts. | |

The captain and covering sergeant take the same positions, and are recalled into line in the same way, in *all* the firings. A *roll* of the drum and a *tap* are substituted, when cartridges are employed, for the last two commands, and, in that

| Explanations. | Commands | |
|---|---|---|
| | of Instructor. | of Capt. or Lt. |

case, the file-closers repeat the command, *Cease firing.*

| | | |
|---|---|---|
| The captains will sometimes command, before AIM............ | ............ | *Right* (or *left*) *oblique.* |
| And sometimes after AIM ................. | ............ | *Recover* ARMS. |

### The fire by file.

| | | |
|---|---|---|
| The instructor...... | 1. *Fire by file.* | |
| The captain and covering sergeant take post as in the fire by company............... | 2. *Company.* 3. READY. 4. *Commence firing.* | |
| The fire begins on the right. | | |
| The first file fires, and the second aims as the pieces of the first are brought down to reload. This progression applies only to the *first* discharge. | | |
| To stop the firing... | *Cease firing* (or *Roll.*) | *Cease firing.* |
| To recall captain and sergeant............. | POSTS (or Tap.) | |

| EXPLANATIONS. | COMMANDS | |
|---|---|---|
| | OF INSTRUCTOR. | OF CAPT. OR LT. |

### The fire by rank.

| | | |
|---|---|---|
| The instructor commands............ Captain and covering sergeant take posts... | 1. *Fire by rank.* 2. *Company.* 3. READY. 4. *Rear rank. Aim.* 5. FIRE. 6. LOAD. | |
| After one or two pieces in the rear rank are at a ready........ | 1. *Front rank.* 2. AIM. 3. FIRE. 4. LOAD. | |
| The fire alternates between the ranks till the signal to cease firing. The fire may be *oblique*, and pieces may be recovered as in the fire by company. | | |

### The fire by the rear rank.

| | | |
|---|---|---|
| The instructor...... The captain places | 1. *Face by the rear rank.* | |

## THE FIRE BY THE REAR RANK.

| EXPLANATIONS. | COMMANDS | |
|---|---|---|
| | OF INSTRUCTOR. | OF CAPT. OR LT. |
| himself one pace in front of the right file facing to it, the covering sergeant one pace behind him. The file-closers pass through the captain's interval, and in rear of the sergeant, posting themselves opposite their places in line, and facing to the rear................ | 2. *Company.* 3. *About— Face.* | |
| The captain and sergeant post themselves in the interval, after the company faces about. The captain in the rear (now front) rank, covered by the sergeant in the front (now rear) rank. | | |
| The fires are executed as by the front rank, and by the same commands. The *fire by file* commences on the (now) right, and that *by rank* with the (now) rear rank. | | |

## THE FIRE BY THE REAR RANK.

| EXPLANATIONS. | COMMANDS | |
|---|---|---|
| | OF INSTRUCTOR. | OF CAPT. OR LT. |
| To bring back the company to its proper front.................. | 1. *Face by the front rank.* <br> 2. *Company.* <br> 3. *About—* FACE. | |
| The captain, covering sergeant, and file-closers execute all that has been said for facing by the rear rank. | | |

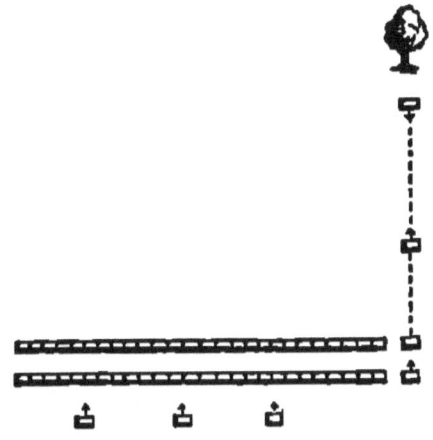

TO ADVANCE IN LINE OF BATTLE.

## TO ADVANCE IN LINE OF BATTLE.

| Explanations. | Commands | |
|---|---|---|
| | Of Instructor. | Of Capt. or Lt. |

### THIRD LESSON.

#### To advance in line of battle.

| | | |
|---|---|---|
| The instructor throws himself twenty-five or thirty paces in front, faces to the captain and covering sergeant, places himself on their direction, and then commands... | 1. *Company—* Forward. | |
| A sergeant, previously designated, places himself six paces in advance of the captain, and is assured in the direction by the instructor to whom he faces, after which this sergeant takes points on the ground in the right line which, drawn from himself, would pass between the heels of the instructor, who commands............. | 2. March. | |

The men take the touch of the elbows toward the side of the directing sergeant; the one next to the captain marches a little in rear of him, preserving the line of his shoulders parallel with his. The captain marches in the trace of the directing

| Explanations. | Commands | |
|---|---|---|
| | OF INSTRUCTOR. | OF CAPT. OR LT. |

sergeant, keeping the distance of six paces between them.

If the men lose the step, the instructor commands *To the* STEP, at which they recover it by a glance at the directing sergeant.

The captain and directing sergeant may be placed either on the right or left flank, and the ranks may be either *opened* or *closed*.

## To halt and align the company.

| | | |
|---|---|---|
| The instructor commands............. | 1. *Company.* 2. HALT. | |
| The directing sergeant remains in front, unless ordered to retire. | | |

If the alignment is very defective, the instructor advances two or four files, on the side of direction for a basis, and aligns the company on it.

| | | |
|---|---|---|
| But if it be not so he simply commands...... | | *Captain rectify the alignment.* |
| The captain directs this or that file *forward*, or back, in the front, and the covering sergeant does the same in the rear rank. | | |

## OBLIQUE MARCH IN LINE OF BATTLE.

| EXPLANATIONS. | COMMANDS. | |
|---|---|---|
| | OF INSTRUCTOR. | OF CAPT. OR LT. |

### Oblique march in line of battle.

| | | |
|---|---|---|
| The company being in the direct march.... | 1. *Right* (or *left*) *oblique.* 2. MARCH. | |
| The directing sergeant maintains his shoulders squarely in oblique line. The captain conforms his march to that of the sergeant. The men in the rear rank march in rear of the man next to their file leaders, dressing toward the side on which the oblique is made. | | |
| To resume the direct march................ | 1. *Forward.* 2. MARCH. | |
| The company ceases to oblique, and marches direct. | | |
| The instructor, from a point twenty paces in front of the captain, rectifies the direction, if needed, of the directing sergeant. | | |

| Explanations. | Commands | |
|---|---|---|
| | Of Instructor. | Of Capt. or Lt. |

The oblique may be either to the side of direction, or to the other side. In either case the guide is, during the oblique march, on that side to which the company obliques.

| | | |
|---|---|---|
| To mark time........ | 1. *Mark time.*<br>2. MARCH. | |
| To resume the march | 1. *Forward.*<br>2. MARCH. | |
| To take the double-quick step.......... | 1. *Double-quick*<br>2. MARCH. | |
| To pass from double-quick to quick time... | 1. *Quick time.*<br>2. MARCH. | |
| Fifteen or twenty steps at a time may be taken in the back step by the command...... | 1. *Company backward.*<br>2. MARCH. | |

## The march in retreat.

| | | |
|---|---|---|
| The company being at a halt............. | 1. *Company.*<br>2. *About—*FACE. | |
| The instructor places himself twenty-five or thirty paces in front, | | |

| Explanations. | Commands | |
|---|---|---|
| | of Instructor. | of Capt. or Lt. |

faced to the covering sergeant, and on the direction of this sergeant and the captain. ......   1. *Company, Forward.*

The covering sergeant goes into the rank of file-closers, the captain into the place quitted by the sergeant. The directing sergeant places himself six paces in advance of the line of file-closers, and is assured on the direction, as in the advance in line.............   2. MARCH.

The march is executed as when faced by the front rank. The company returns to its proper front, by the same commands, as above, the captain and covering sergeant resuming their habitual places. The only difference is, that the directing sergeant retires at once without an order.

The company marching in line, whether in advance or retreat, the instructor may pass from one to the other by the command. ...........   1. *Company.*
2. *Right about.*
3. MARCH.

## THE MARCH IN RETREAT. 47

| Explanations. | Commands | |
|---|---|---|
| | OF INSTRUCTOR. | OF CAPT. OR LT. |
| The directing sergeant will take his place promptly, assured on his direction by the instructor. In all other respects the movement is executed as if it had been begun from a halt. | | |
| If, instead of 3. *March* above, the instructor commands............ | 3. *Halt.* | |
| The company faces about in marching, and then halts. In other respects, it is as if it had first halted and then faced about. | | |
| The company will march in line, in advance, and retreat, and obliquely, by the command............... preceded by the same command............ as in *quick* time. | 1. *Double-quick.*<br>2. MARCH. | |

If the pieces are shifted to the right shoulder, the rear rank, by shortening the first steps, will increase its distance, if in *quick* time, to sixteen inches, and if in *double-quick* to twenty-six inches. At the command, *halt*, the pieces are brought to

# THE MARCH BY THE FLANK.

| EXPLANATIONS. | COMMANDS ||
|---|---|---|
| | OF INSTRUCTOR. | OF CAPT. OR LT. |

the shoulder, and the rear rank closes to thirteen inches. If the pieces are *trailed* at the *double-quick*, they are to be *shouldered*, when the company halts—the same as when the time is quick and the pieces at a support.

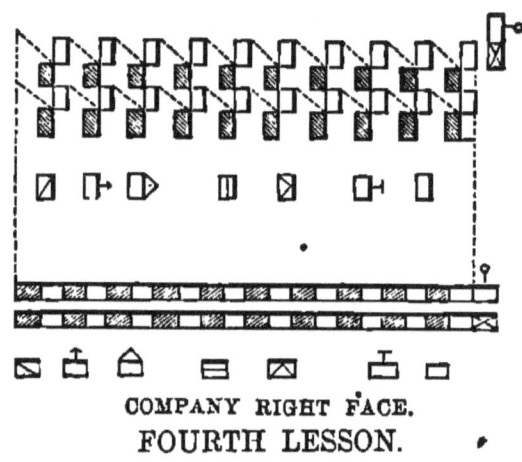

COMPANY RIGHT FACE.

## FOURTH LESSON.

### The march by the flank.

| | |
|---|---|
| The company being in line, and at a halt.. | 1. *Company, right*—FACE. |
| The whole having faced, the files double, the rear rank men and file-closers taking a side | |

## THE MARCH BY THE FLANK.

| EXPLANATIONS. | COMMANDS | |
|---|---|---|
| | OF INSTRUCTOR. | OF CAPT. OR LT. |
| step to the right. The captain and covering sergeant take a side step to the left, so that the sergeant may be in front of the first man of the front rank, and the captain on the left of the sergeant. | | |
| To move forward... | 2. *Forward.* 3. MARCH. | |

The company faces to the left by substituting *left* for *right*, above. The left guide places himself before the leading man of the front rank, the captain on the guide's right, and the right guide behind the last man of the front rank.

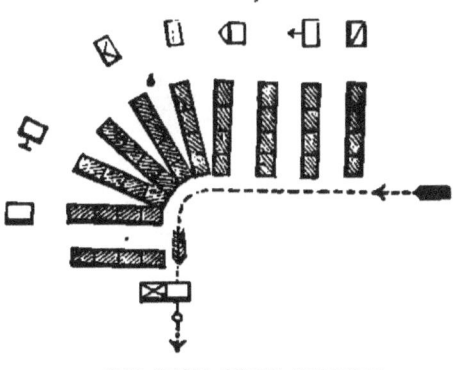

BY FILE LEFT MARCH.

## CHANGING FILES.

| Explanations. | Commands ||
| --- | --- | --- |
| | Of Instructor. | Of Capt. or Lt. |

### To change direction by file.

The company marching by the right flank, or at a halt.......... 
1. *By file left (or right.)*
2. MARCH.

To whichever side the turn is made the man on the inside shortens five or six of his steps; and the one on the outside takes steps of the usual length. Both describe an arc of a circle. The touch of elbows is always to the side of the front rank man.

### To halt the company and face it to the front.

The instructor commands..............
1. *Company.*
2. *Halt.*
3. FRONT.

The company faces to the *left*, if it had been faced by the right flank, and *vice versa.* In both

| Explanations. | Commands | |
|---|---|---|
| | Of Instructor. | Of Capt. or Lt. |
| cases the files undouble and the rear rank and file-closers close to their distance, the captain and the two guides retake their places as in line of battle. | | |

### Doubling and undoubling files.

| | | |
|---|---|---|
| The company, in line of battle and marching to the front, the instructor may command*....... | 1. *Company by the right flank.* 2. HALT. | |
| The company will face in marching halt, and immediately double the files. | | |
| The company may be halted by the *left* flank, on the same principle. | | |
| The company marching by the right (or left) flank, the instructor may command........ | 1. *Company by the left (or right) flank.* 2. HALT. | |

---

* Casey's Tactics. The practice of these movements will facilitate the doubling and undoubling when in march.

## 52 DOUBLING AND UNDOUBLING FILES.

| Explanations. | Commands | |
|---|---|---|
| | OF INSTRUCTOR. | OF CAPT. OR LT. |
| The company will face to the front (or rear) in marching, halt, and undouble files. | | |
| If in facing to the *right* or *left* the company becomes faced to the *rear*, the numbers undouble so as never to *intervert* the order of the two kinds of numbers in the *rank*: that is, if the rank were to be then *faced about*, the order of the numbers, counting from the same flank is the same. (If the face is *from* the *right flank face* to the rear, the odd step up to the left of the even numbers. If from the *left flank face*, to the rear, the even step up to the right of the odd numbers.) | | |
| But, being in any way faced to the rear then facing to either flank, the doubling is precisely the reverse of what takes place when facing from the front. For example, the company being faced to the rear, when the command is given by the instructor............ | 1. By the *left flank*. 2. HALT (or 2. MARCH). | |
| The company faces to its left, and the even numbers place themselves on the *left* of the odd. | | |
| If, instead, the in- | | |

## TO FORM THE COMPANY.

| EXPLANATIONS. | COMMANDS ||
| --- | --- | --- |
| | OF INSTRUCTOR. | OF CAPT. OR LT. |
| ...structor............ | 1. *By the right flank.* <br> 2. HALT. <br> (or 2 MARCH). | |
| The odd numbers place themselves to the *right* of the even numbers.* | | |
| If, in facing to the right or left in marching, the company becomes faced to the rear, the captain places himself two paces in rear of the centre, and the guides pass into the leading rank. | | |

*Note.* "The movements of doubling and un-doubling when passing from the flank march to the front march, ought not to be too precipitate, in order to avoid confusion."—*French Ordonnance*, 1861.

**To form the company on the right or left by file into line.**

| | | |
| --- | --- | --- |
| The company marching by the right flank. | 1. *On the right by file into line.* <br> 2. MARCH. | |

---

* Otherwise the position of the guides would be deranged.

5*

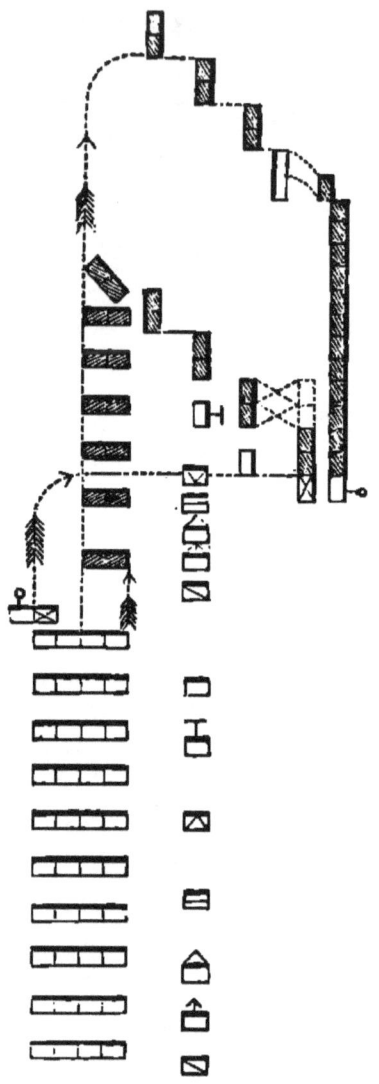

## TO FORM THE COMPANY BY FILE INTO LINE.

| EXPLANATIONS. | COMMANDS | |
|---|---|---|
| | OF INSTRUCTOR. | OF CAPT. OR LT. |
| The rear rank marks time (doubled). The captain and covering sergeant turn to the right, march forward, and are halted by the instructor at six paces | | |

at the least, beyond the rank of file-closers. The captain places himself on the alignment for the front rank, the covering sergeant on that for the rear rank, and behind the captain, each directing the alignment of his rank as their men arrive on it. The first file of the front rank, having continued the march, wheel to the right so soon as they have passed the sergeant, march abreast toward the line, at two paces from it undouble, by the even numbers shortening his step for the odd number to pass before him; the latter inching to the right places himself on the captain's left, and the even number obliquing to the left takes his place on the left of the odd number. The next two of the front-rank men pass beyond the last two, turn to the right, and arrive on the line in the same manner, and so on, in succession, to the left of the rank. The rear-rank men, doubled, execute the same thing, taking care to mark time till they see four men of the front rank on the line, and to cover accurately their file leaders.

Marching by the left flank the formation follows the same principles, *left* being substituted for *right*

56 THE COMPANY MARCHING BY THE FLANK.

| Explanations. | Commands | |
|---|---|---|
| | OF INSTRUCTOR. | OF CAPT. OR LT. |

in the command above. It is the odd number that shortens his step, and the even that precedes, in undoubling on the line. The captain and left guide remain at the left, till the instructor directs them to take their posts in line of battle. The instructor should be placed opposite the right (or left) file to mark the basis of alignment, and, that done should pass along the front, to observe the files as they arrive on the line.

**The company marching by the flank to form company or platoon, and to face them in marching.**

The company marching by the *right* flank, the instructor orders the captain to form it into line who, facing to his company, commands........  ..........  1. *By company into line.*
The covering sergeant marches straight on. The men advance the right shoulder, take the double-quick step, undoubling the files, and by the shortest route place themselves on the alignment of the sergeant, taking the step from him. The rear-rank men follow their file leaders. The 2. MARCH.

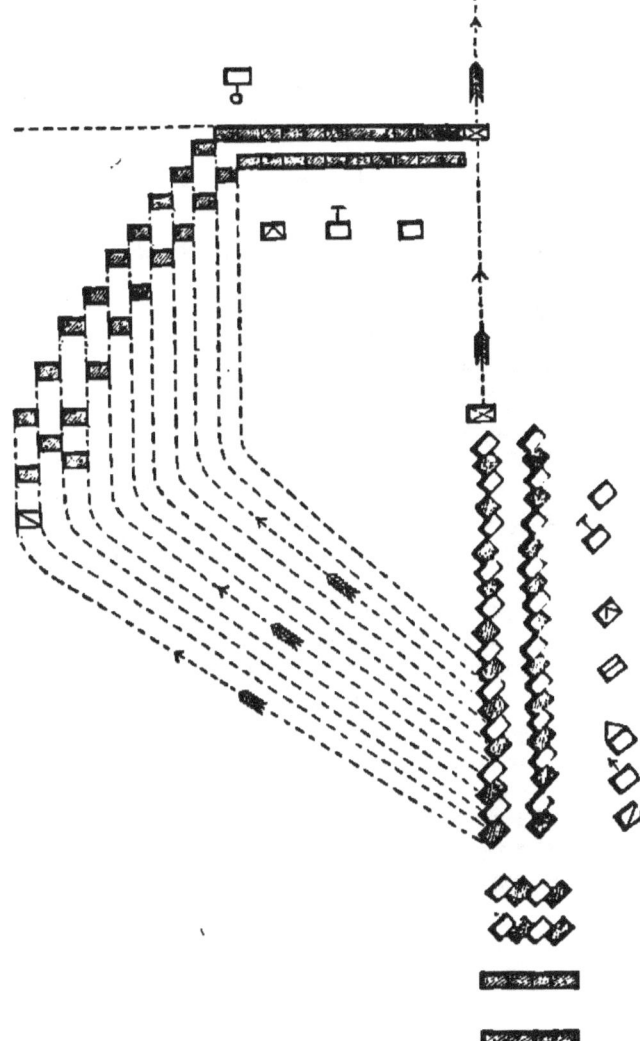

## 58 THE COMPANY MARCHING BY THE FLANK.

| Explanations. | Commands | |
|---|---|---|
| | Of Instructor. | Of Capt. or Lt. |
| company formed, in line, the captain commands............ The left guide places himself on the left of the front rank, and the captain two paces in front of the centre. | ............ | *Guide left.* |

If the company is marching by the *left* flank, the commands and means of execution are the same, and the last command is *guide right*, when the covering sergeant becomes the guide, the second sergeant remaining on the left of the front rank.

In a company which is, or is supposed to be, part of a column, these two sergeants are always posted as above, and one or other is charged with the direction. They are styled *right* and *left guide* respectively. If (marching by either flank) the company had *faced about* before coming into line, the files so undouble that numbers one and two of the front rank arrive on the line together and abreast, the rear-rank men of their group obliquing to cover them in file.

The instructor wishing to form platoons, instead of company as above, gives the order to the captain, who,

THE COMPANY MARCHING BY THE FLANK. 59

| Explanations. | Commands | |
|---|---|---|
| | of Instructor. | of Capt. or Lt. |
| facing to the company, | ............ | 1. *By platoon, into line.* |
| | | 2. **March.** |
| The captain places himself before the centre of the first platoon, the first-lieutenant passing by its right flank before that of the second. the men move, into line as in the last instance, the platoons formed, each chief commands................ | ............ | *Guide left.* |
| At this, the first sergeant passing rapidly along the front, places himself on the left of his platoon, and the second sergeant takes the left of the second. | | |

When the march is by the left flank the principles are the same. Both the captain and first-lieutenant pass around the left of the company, each to place himself in front of his platoon; each gives the command, *guide right*, and it is the guide of the *second* platoon that passes to its right.

All these movements may be executed by direct commands of the instructor.

The instructor will exercise the company in passing from the front to the flank march, and re-

| Explanations. | Commands | |
|---|---|---|
| | of Instructor. | of Capt. or Lt. |
| ciprocally, by the commands............. | 1. *Company by the (right or left)* <br> 2. March. | |
| Being in column by platoon, the platoons may be marched by their right or left flanks by the same commands. At the first command the chiefs and guides will shift to the indicated flank. | | |
| The instructor may likewise face about the column in marching by the commands........ | 1. *Company right about.* <br> 2. March (or 2. Halt). | |
| Adding, in the first case.............. | *Guide right* (or *left*). | |
| Marching in column by platoon, the march may be continued in the same direction, the right in front by the command, | 1. *Company by the right flank.* <br> 2. *By file left.* <br> 3. March. | |
| The chief and guide of the second platoon pass through the interval to their places as file-closers, just before they have conducted | | |

| EXPLANATIONS. | COMMANDS | |
|---|---|---|
| | OF INSTRUCTOR. | OF CAPT. OR LT. |
| the right of their platoon to unite with the left of the first. With the left in front | 1. *Company by the left flank.* 2. *By file right.* 3. MARCH. | |
| The principle is the same. A step before the first unites with the second platoon, the first sergeant returns to his place in the rear, and the captain takes the place of the first-lieutenant, who retires to his place as a file-closer. | | |

## FIFTH LESSON.

### To break into column by platoon.

| | | |
|---|---|---|
| The company being in line and at a halt... | 1. *By platoon, right wheel.* | |
| The captain and first-lieutenant place themselves two paces before | | |

62   TO BREAK INTO COLUMN BY PLATOON.

| Explanations. | Commands | |
|---|---|---|
| | OF INSTRUCTOR. | OF CAPT. OR LT. |

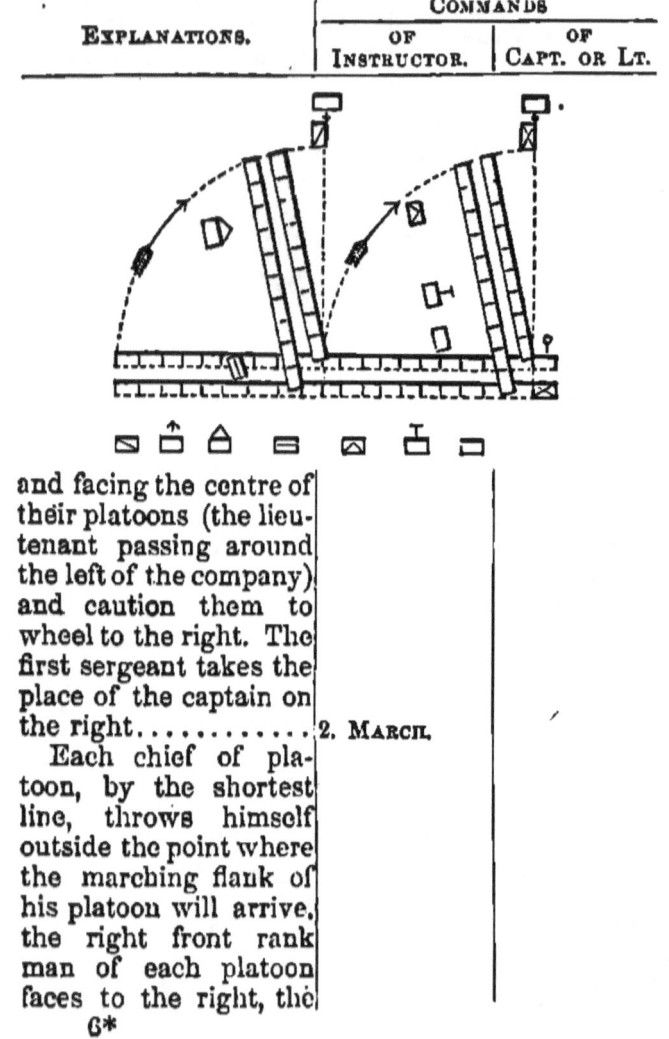

and facing the centre of their platoons (the lieutenant passing around the left of the company) and caution them to wheel to the right. The first sergeant takes the place of the captain on the right............ | 2. MARCH.

Each chief of platoon, by the shortest line, throws himself outside the point where the marching flank of his platoon will arrive, the right front rank man of each platoon faces to the right, the

6*

## TO BREAK INTO COLUMN BY PLATOON. 63

| EXPLANATIONS. | COMMANDS | |
|---|---|---|
| | OF INSTRUCTOR. | OF CAPT. OR LT. |
| first sergeant standing fast. The platoons wheel on a' fixed pivot. When the moving flank shall be three paces from the perpendicular each chief of platoon.. | ... ........ | 1. *Platoon.* 2. HALT. |
| The first and second sergeants go to the left of their platoons, are placed on the line of the man who had faced the chief of platoon step back two paces... | ............ | 3. *Left,* DRESS. FRONT. |
| The alignment ended, the chiefs take their posts, two paces in front of the centre of their platoons. To BREAK TO THE LEFT................. | ............ | 1. *By platoon, left wheel.* 2. MARCH. 3. *Right.* DRESS. 4. FRONT. |
| To break by platoon and *not to halt* after the wheel.............. (The instructor cautioning the company not to halt.) | ............ | 1. *By platoon, right wheel.* |

| Explanations. | Commands | |
|---|---|---|
| | of Instructor. | of Capt. or Lt. |
| The chiefs throw themselves before the centres of the platoons and caution them to move on after wheeling, the covering sergeant replaces the captain... | ............ | 2. March. |
| The platoons wheel on a fixed pivot, the right front rank marks time in turning. The marching flank arrived nearly at the perpendicular......... | ............ | 3. *Forward*. 4. March. |
| The men step out in the full step. ......... | ............ | 5. *Guide left*. |
| The guides place themselves on the left flanks. The men touch elbows toward the left. | | |

If the company be in march by the front, it will break, by platoon in the same manner, the pivot man marking time.

The company may be broken to the left, in the same manner, the indication then being, *left wheel.*

| Explanations. | Commands | |
|---|---|---|
| | Of Instructor. | Of Capt. or Lt. |

To march in column.

The column, being right in front (*i. e.* the first platoon leading) the instructor throws himself twenty-five or thirty paces in front of the leading guide and facing to him, the guide takes points in the line which passes through the heels of that officer, who then commands...

1. *Column forward.*
2. *Guide left.*
3. March.

March.

The chiefs of platoon repeat the last command.

The men touch elbows toward the guide, the man next to him will take care never to march beyond him, and not to touch elbows with him, but to preserve an interval of six inches between them. The rear guide follows

## TO CHANGE DIRECTION.

| EXPLANATIONS. | COMMANDS | |
|---|---|---|
| | OF INSTRUCTOR. | OF CAPT. OR LT. |
| the trace of the one in front. If the latter is directed to incline at a given point, the rear guide makes the same change of direction when he arrives at the same point. The chiefs see that the platoons conform to the guides. | | / |

The guides are to preserve the direction, step, and distance, of which the last is the most important.

In column, chiefs of subdivision repeat the commands *march* and *halt*, likewise when the column moves to form line, but not *vice versa*.

A column left in front, takes the guide to the *right*, that is all the difference that there is in the commands and execution.

### To change direction.

The change of direction, in column, is always made by a wheel, on a movable pivot. The guide is taken therefore to the side *opposite* that wheeled toward. If it is wished that a column right in front change direction to the left, the instructor commands *guide right*, and goes himself or sends a marker to the intended point, which is taken on the side of the guide, who directs himself so as to

## TO CHANGE DIRECTION. 67

| EXPLANATIONS. | COMMANDS ||
| | OF INSTRUCTOR. | OF CAPT. OR LT. |

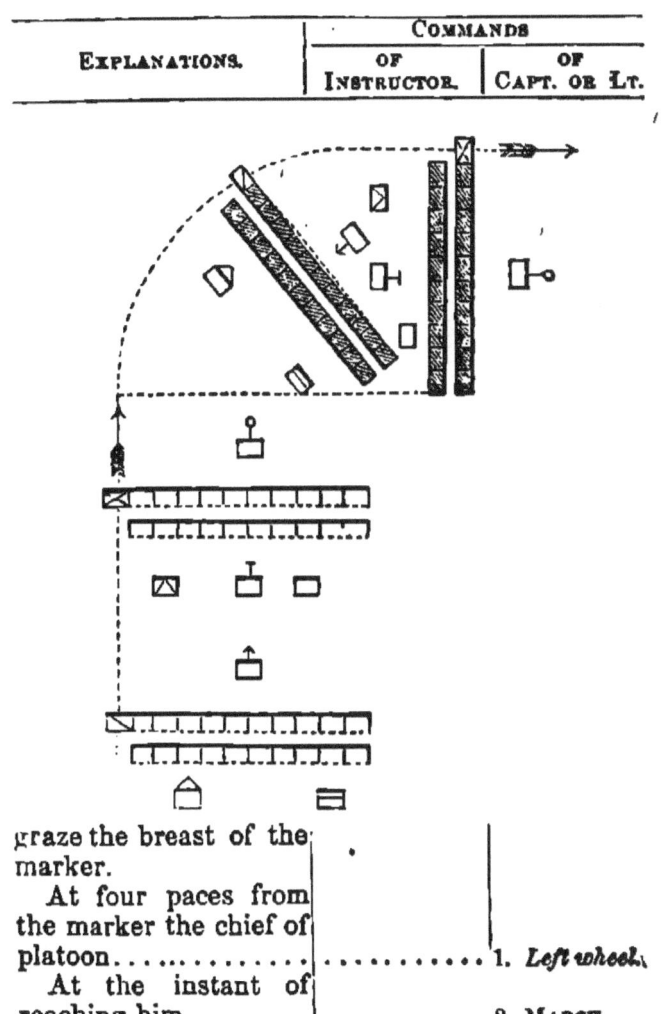

graze the breast of the marker.

At four paces from the marker the chief of platoon.............. | .............1. *Left wheel.*

At the instant of reaching him......... | ............2. **MARCH.**

## TO CHANGE DIRECTION.

| EXPLANATIONS. | COMMANDS | |
|---|---|---|
| | OF INSTRUCTOR. | OF CAPT. OR LT. |
| The pivot takes steps of nine inches if in *quick* time, and of eleven if the time be *double-quick*, and the wheel being completed...... when the platoon marches directly forward, and the instructor adds............ | ............ *Guide left.* | 3. *Forward.* 4. MARCH. |
| Habitually, light infantry in column, changes direction in marching by a *wheel*, and to the side opposite to the guide. When required, the change may be made to the side of the guide, not by wheeling, but by *turning*, as follows: The company being in column of platoons, (or itself being supposed to form a subdivision of a column), and in march, right in front, the instructor, causing first the point of change of direction to be marked, on the side and in advance of the guide, commands............ | *Head of column to the left* (or *right*.) | |
| The chief of the leading subdivision, when the guide is within four paces of the marker, commands.... and when the guide is | ............ | 1. *Left turn* (or *right turn.*) |

## TO HALT THE COLUMN. 69

| EXPLANATIONS. | COMMANDS | |
|---|---|---|
| | OF INSTRUCTOR. | OF CAPT. OR LT. |
| precisely opposite the marker............ The guide turns at right angles, without changing the step, takes points in the new direction and marches forward. The following subdivision (if there be one) turns at the same point, by the same commands from its chief. The files come into line, as in the movement of, *By company into line.* | ............. | 2. MARCH. |

The change of direction with the left in front is on the same principle. If the change is to the right, the guide is shifted to the left before the wheel, and after it, the command is given, *Guide right.* If the change is to the right, with the right in front, or to the left with the left in front, no change of guide is necessary.

### To halt the column.

| | | |
|---|---|---|
| The instructor commands............. | 1. *Column.* 2. HALT. | HALT. |
| Promptly repeated by the chiefs of platoon. | | |

70 TO FORM TO THE RIGHT OR LEFT INTO LINE.

| Explanations. | Commands | |
|---|---|---|
| | Of Instructor. | Of Capt. or Lt. |

**Being in column, to form to the right or left into line.**

The column being at a halt, and right in front, the instructor places himself at platoon distance in front of the leading guide, facing to him, and rectifies, if necessary, the position of the guide of the second platoon; he then commands....... *Left*—Dress.

Chiefs of platoons step to the left flanks, align them on the guides and command......... .................. Front. and take their posts in column.

The instructor...... 1. *Left into line, wheel.*
2. March. March.

## TO FORM TO THE RIGHT OR LEFT INTO LINE.

| Explanations. | Commands |  |
|---|---|---|
| | Of Instructor. | Of Capt. or Lt. |
| The guides stand fast, the left front-rank man of each platoon faces to the left, the chiefs turn to their platoons, which wheel on a fixed pivot, and command... giving the last command when the marching flank is three paces from the line of battle. The lieutenant passing by the left flank takes his post as a file-closer, the captain from the right.................. aligning the company on the left front-rank man, while the right front rank man places his breast against the left arm of the instructor. | .............. .............. | 1. *Platoon.* 2. Halt. *Right*—Dress. |
| The captain commands.............. and the instructor..... | .............. *Guides*—Posts | Front. |
| The first sergeant covers the captain, and the second takes his place as file-closer. | | |

## TO FORM TO THE RIGHT OR LEFT INTO LINE.

| EXPLANATIONS. | COMMANDS ||
|---|---|---|
| | OF INSTRUCTOR. | OF CAPT. OR LT. |

If the column were left in front, the command would be, *Right into line, wheel;* the company would be aligned by the captain from its left, who at the command *Guides*—POSTS, would take his place on the right.

If the column is in march, and it is wished to wheel directly into line and then to halt, but not to halt in column, the instructor......

| | |
|---|---|
| *Left* (or *right*) *into line wheel.* | |
| 2. MARCH. | MARCH. |

and throws himself to platoon distance in front of the leading guide.

At the command MARCH, the guides halt, the platoons wheel, and the company is aligned, in all respects as before.

Being in march in column, when it is wished to wheel into line, without halting at all (either in column or line) the instructor commands.....

| | |
|---|---|
| 1. *By platoons left* (or *right*) *wheel.* | |
| 2. MARCH. | MARCH. |

The guides *halt* at the command *March*, the man next to them *marks time* in turning,

## TO BREAK INTO PLATOONS AND TO RE-FORM. 73

| EXPLANATIONS. | COMMANDS | |
|---|---|---|
| | OF INSTRUCTOR. | OF CAPT. OR LT. |
| the platoons wheel on a fixed pivot, and when nearly in line, the instructor adds.......... | 3. *Forward.* 4. MARCH. | |
| The company step out, the officers and guides take their proper posts............... | 5. *Guide right* (or *left.*) | |
| The captain and covering sergeant shift to the designated flank, if not already there, and the directing sergeant places himself six paces in advance, and is rectified by the instructor *from the front.* | | |

## SIXTH LESSON.

### To break into platoons and to re-form the company.

The company being in march, as part of a column right in front, the instructor gives the order to the captain, who facing to the company, commands............ | ....... .... | 1. *Break into platoons.*

74 TO BREAK INTO PLATOONS AND TO RE-FORM.

| Explanations. | Commands | |
|---|---|---|
| | OF INSTRUCTOR. | OF CAPT. OR LT. |

and then places himself before the centre of the first platoon. The first lieutenant, passing around the left flank, places himself in front of the second, and commands.................. ............... *Mark time.*
The captain adds..... ............... 2. *March.*
 The first sergeant,

## TO BREAK INTO PLATOONS AND TO RE-FORM. 75

| EXPLANATIONS. | COMMANDS | |
|---|---|---|
| | OF INSTRUCTOR. | OF CAPT. OR LT. |
| passing along the front, places himself on the left of the first platoon which marches directly forward, the second platoon marks time, its chief, so soon as it can pass, commands...... | ............ | 1. *Right oblique.* <br> 2. MARCH. |
| The second platoon, shortening the step, obliques, and at the moment that its guide is nearly on the direction of the guide of the first, the lieutenant adds... | ............ | 1. *Forward.* <br> 2. MARCH. |

In a column left in front, the means are inverse. The second platoon marches on, while the first obliques, while it is the left guide who passes to the right flank of the second (now leading) platoon, the right guide remaining at the right of the first.

To form the company, the right being in front, the instructor gives the direction to the captain, who commands......

| | | *Form company.* <br> 1. *First platoon.* <br> 2. *Right oblique.* |
|---|---|---|
| The chief of the second cautions it to march directly on........... | ............ | 3. MARCH. |
| The lieutenant repeats................ | ............ | (MARCH.) |

## 76 TO BREAK INTO PLATOONS AND TO RE-FORM.

| Explanations. | Commands of Instructor. | Commands of Capt. or Lt. |
|---|---|---|
| The first platoon obliques, its guide shifts to its right flank, when it has nearly unmasked the second platoon, its chief adds............ at the instant of unmasking. | ............. | 1. *Mark time*, and 2. March. |
| So soon as the second platoon shall be nearly in line with the first, the captain commands.. | ............. | Forward. |
| The lieutenant retires, and at the instant the platoons unite, the captain adds............. At which they step out together. | ............. | March. |

In a column left in front the company is formed by inverse means, applying to the second (then leading) platoon what has been said of the first, and reciprocally. The guide of the second passes to its left flank, the guide of the first remains at its right, the chief of the second commands *Forward*, and the captain, March.

The movements of breaking and forming company may be executed by the instructor's direct

| EXPLANATIONS. | COMMANDS | |
|---|---|---|
| | OF INSTRUCTOR. | OF CAPT. OR LT. |

commands, which would be the same as those given above by the captain.*

### To break files to the rear, and to bring them again into line.

Files are to be so broken that, whereas they were marching by the front, they shall be marching in the same direction by the flank. The files broken off must so cover in file that they may either come back to the front, or unite with the other files in the march by the opposite flank. Whatever the mode adopted, the files broken off must, in effect, *double*, and gain the rear of the nearest files that continue in line. The method prescribed in General Casey's Tactics seems so superior to others, that it will be preferred here. His principle is, to apply to files what is performed by a subdivision at the command, 1. *By the right (or left) flank.* 2. *By file left (or right.)*

The instructor gives the direction to the captain, who turning to his company, which is marching in

---

* It is obvious that the movements in the text oblige the column to deviate to the right when the right is in front, and to the left when the left is. If the *following* platoon should oblique into line, in the double-quick step, (on the principle of the passage of obstacles in the battalion manœuvres) the inconvenience would be avoided.
J. M.

78    TO BREAK FILES TO THE REAR.

| Explanations. | Commands | |
|---|---|---|
| | of Instructor. | of Capt. or Lt. |

| | | |
|---|---|---|
| line, and right in front, commands............ | ............ | 1. *Two files from left to rear.*<br>2. **March.** |
| The left group faces to the right, doubles, and wheels by file to the left, covering the | | |

| Explanations. | Commands ||
| | Of Instructor. | Of Capt. or Lt. |
|---|---|---|
| nearest files which have continued to march. The left guide closes in to the flank.<br>If another, or other, groups are ordered to the rear (by the same commands) that, or those, already there | | |

advance the outer shoulder, shorten the step, and gain ground to the right, in order to leave space for the new files, and to cover them in file. The guide as before gradually closes to the flank.

To bring the files back into line, the instructor directs the captain, who facing to the company commands....... ........ ............1. *Two files into line.*
2. March.

The designated files come into line, precisely as files do when the command is, *By company into line.* Those that remain in rear gain ground to the left and close on the flank, the guide opening out to permit the files that enter to pass into line.

The captain faces to the company to superintend the breaking and forming of the files. The in-

| Explanations. | Commands |  |
|---|---|---|
|  | Of Instructor. | Of Capt. or Lt. |

structor is on the flank for the same purpose. If there is an odd file, it must be broken off separately, the doubling and undoubling requiring this. The others are broken by groups (*two, four, six files*) for the same reason. The march demands that files be broken only from the side of *direction* (that of the guide). [It is seen that a section or a plate may be broken off and brought into line, on the same principle.] The file-closers are placed as in other flank marches.

In a column left in front, the principles are the same, the commands and means of execution are inverse.

### The march in column of route.

The habitual rate is one hundred and ten steps in a minute. The company being at a halt, the instructor commands..

1. *Column forward.*
2. *Guide left* (or *right*.)
3. *Route step.*
4. MARCH.

The rear rank, by shortening the first steps, takes the distance of twenty-eight inches from the front rank. The men carry their arms, *at will* (slung, on

| Explanations. | Commands | |
|---|---|---|
| | of Instructor. | of Capt. or Lt. |

either shoulder, &c., but the muzzle always upward). The step is not cadenced, nor is silence preserved in the ranks. Changes of direction are made on a simple intimation from the captain, without a command. The step at the pivot is fourteen inches.

To pass to the cadenced step the instructor will command........ | *Right shoulder shift*—Arms.
1. *Quick time.*
2. March.

The men take the cadenced step and the rear rank closes to sixteen inches from the front.

To pass from the cadenced to the route step the instructor commands . | 1. *Route step.*
2. March.

The rear rank, shortening its step, takes the interval of a pace from the front rank, the arms are *at will.*

## THE MARCH IN COLUMN OF ROUTE.

| EXPLANATIONS. | COMMANDS | |
|---|---|---|
| | OF INSTRUCTOR. | OF CAPT. OR LT. |

| | | |
|---|---|---|
| The company marching by the front in the route step, to march it by the flank in the same direction, the instructor commands........... | 1. *Company by the right* (or *left*) *flank.*<br>2. *By file left* (or *right.*)<br>3. MARCH. | |
| The company faces doubling, and files, the right (or left) guide leading, and the captain on his left (or right). | | |

[Hardee and Casey direct the movement as above. Looking at the fact that the ranks are a pace apart, that they have to double the files, and that the step is not supposed to be regulated, it is a question whether the cadenced step should not be first resumed. Scott's Tactics required that it should be, and the French Ordinance of 1861 prescribes that arms be *shouldered* and the cadenced step resumed as preparatory, which would close the ranks even nearer than in the case of passing from *Route-step*, to *Quick-time*, as seen above.]

The company marching by the front, in the route-step, is broken into platoons, and is re-formed, the same as when marching in the cadenced step, with this single exception, that the chiefs of platoons take the places of the guides, and these fall back into the rear rank.

## THE MARCH IN COLUMN OF ROUTE.

| EXPLANATIONS. | COMMANDS ||
| --- | --- | --- |
| | OF INSTRUCTOR. | OF CAPT. OR LT. |

Platoons may be broken into sections, but *only* in column of route, and not then, unless the platoons have at least *twelve* files, because if there were less than twelve files in the platoons, the column of sections (there being a pace between the ranks) would in marching extend itself beyond its proper depth.

To form sections the instructor gives the order to the captain, who commands .................

The platoons break in the same way that the company breaks into platoons. The captain commands the first section, the second lieutenant the second, the first lieutenant the third and the next in rank the fourth.

Chiefs of sections take the places of their guides, and these fall back into the rear rank.

The file-closers close up to within a pace of the rear rank.

.............. 
1. *Break into sections.*
2. MARCH.

To re-form the platoons the instructor gives the order to the captain,

| Explanations. | Commands | |
|---|---|---|
| | OF INSTRUCTOR. | OF CAPT. OR LT. |
| who commands. Each chief places himself before the centre of his section. | | 1. *Form platoons.* |
| Executed as in forming company. | | 2. MARCH. |
| The platoons formed, the chiefs take the places of their guides, the chiefs of the second and fourth sections return to the rank of file-closers, and this opens out to two paces from the rear-rank. | | |

[In both the foregoing movements, the French Ordinance requires arms to be shouldered, and the cadenced step taken, prior to their execution.]

Marching in column of platoons or sections, the company may be marched in the same direction by the flank, by the commands: 1. *By the right flank.* 2. *By file left, &c.*, as in column by company. Likewise files may be broken off, in the same manner, observing, however, that the *section* must not be reduced below six files, not counting its chief.

The company marching by the flank will double and undouble files on an intimation from the instructor to the captain, who after causing the cadenced step to be resumed and arms to be shoul-

| Explanations. | Commands | |
|---|---|---|
| | OF INSTRUCTOR. | OF CAPT. OR LT. |
| dered or supported, commands............ | ............ | 1. *In two ranks undouble files.* <br> 2. MARCH. |
| If marching by the *right* flank, the odd numbers march on, the even shorten the step and oblique to the left, behind the odd. The rear rank close to the left to touch elbows with the front-rank men. | | |

If the march be by the *left* flank, it is the odd men who oblique behind the even. The company may, in a similar manner, substituting *one rank* for *two ranks* in the command above, be formed from two ranks into one, on the flank march. The files all mark time, except the guide and first man of the front rank, who continue to march; each rear-rank man successively, as room is made, steps in behind his front-rank man, followed promptly by the file-leader of the next file. To pass from single file to double, the captain commands...... ............ 1. *In two ranks double files.* 2. MARCH.

The rear-rank men step out on their right

| Explanations. | Commands | |
|---|---|---|
| | of Instructor. | of Capt. or Lt. |

(or left), and each rank closes on its leader.

Marching by the flank in two ranks, the instructor gives the order to the captain, who commands.................... | .............. | 1. *In four ranks double files.*

The files double as when the company faces from front to flank. | | 2. *March.*

*Before* all these changes in the depth of the files, the company is to be brought to the cadenced step with arms shouldered or supported. *After* them, the instructor causes the route step to be resumed.

In the route step the arms are carried *at will*, muzzles always upward. At the command, *Halt*, the rear rank closes to thirteen inches, and the company shoulders arms.

### Countermarch.

The company being right in front, and at a halt, the instructor commands .............. | 1. *Countermarch.*
| | 2. *Company right*—Face.

The company faces, the guides' face about, the captain goes to the right, breaks two files to the rear, and places

## COUNTERMARCH.

| EXPLANATIONS. | COMMANDS | |
|---|---|---|
| | OF INSTRUCTOR. | OF CAPT. OR LT. |
| himself on the left of the first man of the front rank to conduct him................ | 3. *By file left.* 4. MARCH. | |
| The company wheels by file around the right guide, marches parallel to the guides; at four paces from the left guide the captain commands.............. when directly in rear and two paces behind | ............ | 1. *Company.* |

| Explanations. | Commands | |
|---|---|---|
| | of Instructor. | of Capt. or Lt. |
| the left guide........ | ............ | 2. *Halt.* |
| The captain steps two paces outside of the left guide, and commands.............. | ............ | 3. **Front.** 4. *Right—* **Dress.** |
| The company aligned, the captain adds... and takes his post opposite the centre. The guides exchange places, passing rapidly along the front. | ............ | **Front.** |

With the left in front, the means and commands are inverse, the subdivisions of an open column right in front, countermarching by the right flank, and left in front by the left flank. Platoons may be countermarched on the same principle.

### To form column by platoon on the right or left into line.

| | | |
|---|---|---|
| The column of platoons being right in front and in march, the instructor commands........... | | 1. *On the right into line.* 2. *Guide right.* |
| The guides shift to the right flank. | | |
| The instructor throws himself to the front on the right of the guides | | |

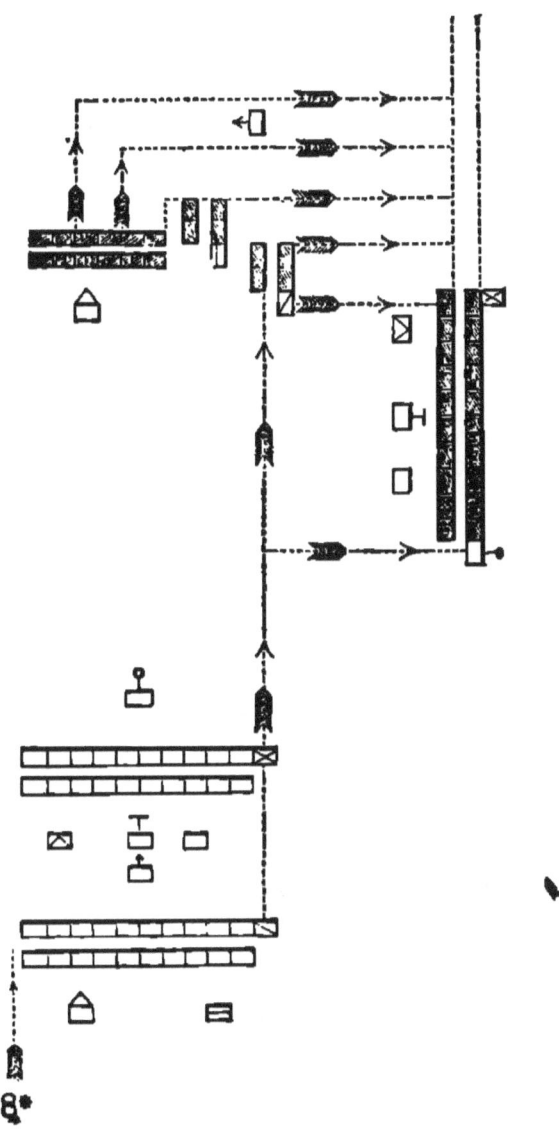

## 90 TO FORM COLUMN BY PLATOON INTO LINE.

| EXPLANATIONS. | COMMANDS | |
| --- | --- | --- |
| | OF INSTRUCTOR. | OF CAPT. OR LT. |
| ten paces, at least, and faced toward the point of direction to the left. The first platoon arrived nearly opposite to the instructor, its chief commands............ | ............ | 1. *Right turn.* |
| and when exactly opposite................. | ............ | 2. MARCH. |
| The platoon *turns*, and the guide so conducts it as to bring its right file opposite to the instructor. When near him the chief of platoon commands ... | ............ | 1. *Platoon.* |
| and when but three paces from him adds.. | ............ | 2. HALT. |
| The guide places himself opposite one of the three left files, faces the instructor and is aligned by him. The chief goes to the right and commands...... | ............ | *Right*—DRESS. |
| The men dress up, the files opposite the instructor and guide touching their elbows with the breast. | | |

| EXLANATIONS. | COMMANDS ||
|---|---|---|
| | OF INSTRUCTOR. | OF CAPT. OR LT. |
| The second platoon continues to march till it is opposite the left of the first, when it is marched upon the line by the same commands, its guide directing himself upon the left file of the first. At the command, *Halt*, its guide places himself opposite one of its then left files and is aligned by the instructor, when its chief commands...... and retires by the left, as a file closer. The second platoon aligned, the captain commands and the instructor.... at which the guides take their posts in line. | .... *Guides*, POSTS. | .... *Right*—DRESS. FRONT. |

With the left in front the column is formed on the left into line, by the change of the command to: 1. *On the left into line.* 2. *Guide left.* The chief of the second platoon aligns it to the left, its left front-rank man touching the instructor's right elbow, and retires as file-closer so soon as the first platoon arrives. The captain having halted his platoon aligns it from the left flank of the company, on its right guide, and at the command *Guides*—POSTS, the guides retire, and the captain takes his post on the right.

**Formation of the company from one rank into two ranks, and reciprocally, and from two ranks into four, and reciprocally.**

Under the head of the *route step*, the change in the depth of the files, has been shown when the company is *in march by the flank*. Those that can be executed from a *halt*, and when in *march by the front*, here follow.

| Explanations. | Commands of Instructor. | Commands of Capt. or Lt. |
|---|---|---|
| The company being at a halt, faced to the front, and in one rank, the instructor commands.. | 1. *In two ranks, form company.* 2. *Company right*—FACE. | |
| The company faces, except the right guide, and the man next to him............ ..... | 3. MARCH. | |
| The men who had faced, step off together, the leading man by a step to the right and rear, places himself to cover the man on the right who did *not* face, | | |

| Explanations. | Commands | |
|---|---|---|
| | OF INSTRUCTOR. | OF CAPT. OR LT. |

forming thus the first file; the next following man closes up to the front-rank man of this file, and faces to the front, covered at once by the fourth man, and so on to the left. The steps to the rear must be taken in the *time* of an ordinary step, and the men who close must face to the front in halting, or the following men will be delayed.

The company, formed as above in two ranks, to form it into one rank, the instructor commands .......... 

The right guide faces to the right.

1. *In one rank, form company.*

2. MARCH.

The guide and first file step off together, the guide directing himself on the prolongation of the front rank, the front-rank man of the first file facing to the right in taking the first

## 94 FORMATION FROM ONE RANK INTO TWO RANKS.

| Explanations. | Commands |  |
|---|---|---|
| | Of Instructor. | Of Capt. or Lt. |
| step; the rear-rank man, turning at the same point, follows him: the front-rank man of the second file steps, in turning, immediately after the rear man of the first, followed by his rear-rank man, and so successively to the left. The captain superintends the filing of the company, and when finished, commands............ | ............ | 1. Halt. 2. Front. |
| The file-closers extend their rank, with that of the company.* | | |

Both the foregoing formations may be executed by the *left* of the company. The company must be first faced *about*, the guides placed in the rear-rank, and, the formation finished, faced again to its proper front. The commands are the same in both cases.†

---

\* It would seem to be simpler to face the company by the flank, first, and then let the rear-rank step into their intervals successively.

† So prescribed, but the objection is, that if there were an *odd* man he would be formed on the *right* of the company.

# FROM TWO RANKS INTO FOUR RANKS.

| Explanations. | Commands | |
|---|---|---|
| | of Instructor. | of Capt. or Lt. |

The company being in two ranks, at a halt, and faced to the front, to form it into four ranks, the instructor commands..

1. *In four ranks, form company.*
2. *Company left*—FACE.

The left guide stands fast. The company faces to the left and doubles.

3. MARCH.

The left file faces to the front, the others step off together, each closes to within five inches of the one that precedes it, they halt successively, and face to the front (doubled). The file-closers contract their rank to correspond with the company. The captain supervises the movement.

The company formed in four ranks, the instructor forms it again into two ranks by the command............

1. *In two ranks, form company.*
2. *Company right*—FACE.

## THE COMPANY IN TWO RANKS.

| EXPLANATIONS. | COMMANDS OF INSTRUCTOR. | OF CAPT. OR LT. |
|---|---|---|
| The left guide stands fast, the company faces. The right guide steps off, and the right file of fours, the second file follows so soon as the first has taken its distance, and so on to the left, when the instructor commands......... The company undoubles files. | 8. MARCH. 1. *Company.* 2. HALT. 8. FRONT. | |

**The company in two ranks being in march by the front, and right in front.**

| | | |
|---|---|---|
| The instructor commands ............. The left guide and left file continue the march to the front. The other files half face to the left and double, the step is lengthened | 1. *In four ranks, form company.* 2. *By the left, double files.* 3. MARCH. | |

## THE COMPANY IN TWO RANKS.

| EXPLANATIONS. | COMMANDS | |
| --- | --- | --- |
| | OF INSTRUCTOR. | OF CAPT. OR LT. |
| so as to keep on the alignment of the guide, toward whom the obliquing files close, and each faces to the front, so soon as the interval on its left is closed up, and resumes the direct step. The rear-rank men shorten the first steps to permit the odd numbers to enter the file. | | |
| The company so formed in four ranks, to form it, in the march by the front, into two ranks, the instructor commands . | 1. *In two ranks, form company.* 2. *By the right, undouble files.* 3. MARCH. | |
| The left guide and file continue the march. The other files oblique to the right, lengthening the step in order to keep in line with the guide, when the second file from the left has taken sufficient distance to permit the left file to come into line, the second, half facing, | | |

| Explanations. | Commands | |
|---|---|---|
| | of Instructor. | of Capt. or Lt. |

resumes the direct march, and the left file undoubles into line, and so successively of all the other files, each forming into two ranks, as soon as that next to it resumes the direct step.

The last two movements (as seen above), are made either *from*, or *toward*, the guide, consequently, with the left in front, the commands and means are inverse, *left* being substituted for *right*.

The last four movements may be executed in the *double-quick*.

The *oblique* march is confined to the march by the *front*, and the Tactics do not direct it to be ever begun from a *halt*.

All the marches (except the backward march) of the third, fourth, fifth, and sixth lessons, may be executed in the *double-quick step*, to effect which the cautionary command *Double-quick* precedes the command MARCH.

In the double-quick step the pieces are to be carried either at the *Right shoulder shift*, or at a *Trail*. In the latter case, the command to trail arms, precedes the command *Double-quick*, MARCH. In the former the men shift the pieces to the right shoulder, at the command *Double-quick*.

In wheeling, if in the *quick* time the pivot flank takes steps of nine inches, if in *double-quick*, of eleven (about a third of the step at the marching flank in both cases).

| Explanations. | Commands ||
| | of Captain. | of Lieutenant. |

## ARTICLE I.

### Deployments.

*By skirmishers* is meant light troops deployed in extended order, having intervals between their groups, files, or individual soldiers.

A company may be deployed either *forward*, that is, on a line in advance of the one it occupies, or, by the flank, that is, on the very line it occupies.

### To deploy forward.

The deployment *forward* is made on some designated *file*, which moves directly forward, in the step indicated in the command, while the other files separate from it by oblique lines and in quicker time.

The platoons and sections are to be carefully marked, and the captain will see that the *centre files* of each are designated. (The last has reference to the *rallying* by platoon or section.)

The company being in line, at a halt or in march, to deploy the first platoon on its left file, holding in reserve the second platoon, the captain commands. . . . . . . . . . . . . . . | 1. *First platoon as skirmishers. On the left file take intervals.* |

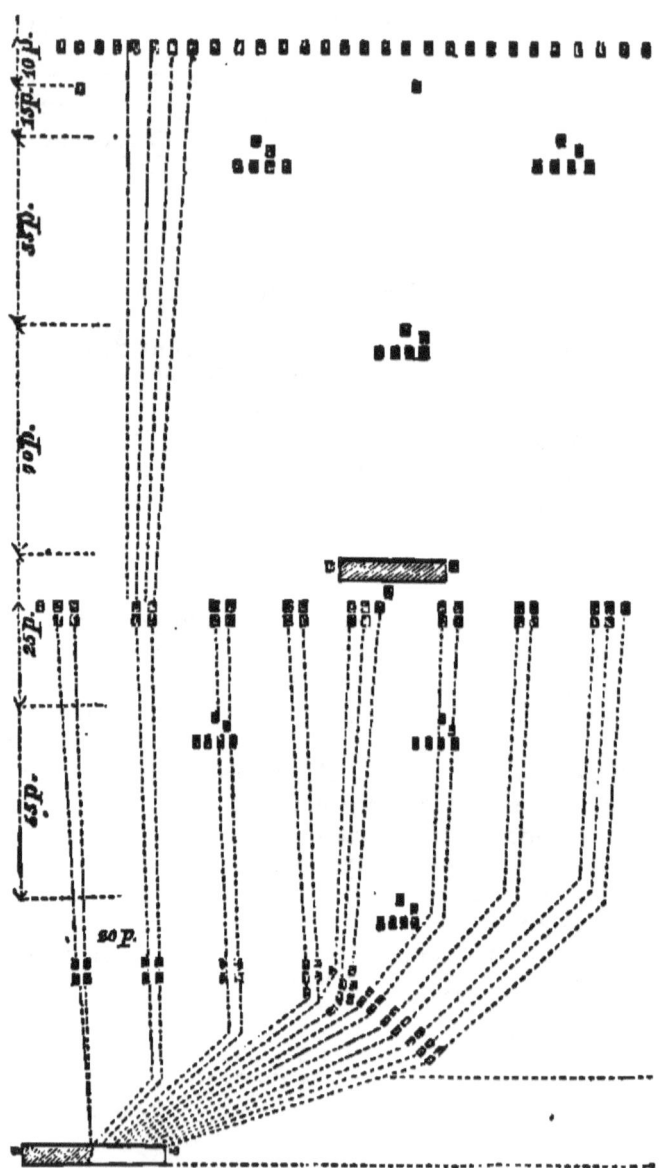

## TO DEPLOY FORWARD.

| EXPLANATIONS. | COMMANDS OF CAPTAIN. | OF LIEUTENANT. |
|---|---|---|
| The first lieutenant places himself in front of the second platoon, and if the company is in march, commands.. If the company is at a halt, the lieutenant commands................ | ............ ............ | *Second platoon*—HALT. *Second platoon backward*— MARCH. |
| The second platoon marches backward three paces, of twenty-eight inches, its chief halts it, the second sergeant places himself on its left, the third on its right. | | |
| At the first command of the captain the second lieutenant places himself two paces behind the centre of the first section, the third lieutenant two paces behind the centre of the second section, the fifth sergeant one pace before the centre of the first platoon, and the fourth sergeant on its left. | | |

9*

## TO DEPLOY FORWARD.

| Explanations. | Commands ||
|---|---|---|
| | Of Captain. | Of Lieutenant. |
| The captain then adds .............. | March (or *Double-quick* —March). | |
| The left group of fours conducted by the fourth sergeant moves directly forward. The other groups extend out to its right, on lines more and more diagonal, moving in quicker time, and as they successively place an interval of twenty paces between themselves and the group nearest them on their left, they turn to the front and march in line with the left group, preserving the intervals. The left guide having reached the point where the left of the line of skirmishers is to rest, the captain commands.............. | *Skirmishers—* Halt. | Halt. |
| The groups not yet in line continue the march till they arrive on it. All the groups deploy, when on the line, into a single rank, each group upon its even-numbered front-rank man, who stands fast, | | |

| Explanations. | Commands ||
|---|---|---|
| | of Captain. | of Lieutenant. |
| his rear-rank man forms on his left five paces distant, the odd-numbered man of the front rank extends to his right ten paces, and the rear man of the odd file is between these two, five paces from | | |

each. Thus when the interval between the groups is twenty paces, the habitual distance between the men of a group being five, the whole line in one extended rank is formed by skirmishers placed at equal intervals of five paces.

The line thus formed, the sergeants fall back ten paces, each in rear of their former posts in line.

Each chief of section, after rectifying the line, falls back twenty-five or thirty paces in rear of the centre of his section; with each of these officers is a group taken from the reserve, and a bugler, who is to repeat the signals of the captain's bugler.

If fired upon, during the deploying, the captain may deploy the groups as they successively gain their proper distances (from the group next on their left).

The captain is eighty paces in rear of the centre of the line, having with him a group of four and a bugler. (The groups with the captain and lieutenants are *deployed* like those in line.)

## TO DEPLOY FORWARD.

| EXPLANATIONS. | COMMANDS ||
|---|---|---|
| | OF CAPTAIN. | OF LIEUTENANT. |

At the beginning of the deployment the first lieutenant faces *about* the second platoon, and marches it to a point one hundred and fifty paces in rear of the centre of the line, holding it at that distance as the reserve.

Where no reserve is required, the entire company can be deployed on the same principle. In this case the first lieutenant commands the second platoon, the second the first, and the fourth and second sections are commanded by the next in rank. The fifth sergeant is the guide of the centre. The lieutenants each have a bugler (but not a group) with them.

The forward deployment may be made on any file of the platoon or company. If the right file be selected as the directing one, the others incline diagonally and extend to the left. If an interior file is the directing one, the groups diverge from it to the right and left, and it is conducted on its right by the fifth sergeant. For example, the captain wishing to deploy on the centre file, commands............... | *Company* (or *First platoon*) *as skirmishers. On the centre file take intervals.*

The fifth sergeant places himself in front to conduct the right

| Explanations. | Commands ||
|---|---|---|
| | OF CAPTAIN. | OF LIEUTENANT. |
| group of fours of the second platoon (or of the second section). | | |

## To deploy by the flank.

| | | |
|---|---|---|
| This deployment can be made only from a halt. The captain commands. | 1. *Second platoon, as skirmishers.* | |
| The first lieutenant places himself two paces behind the centre of the third section, the third lieutenant behind the fourth. The second lieutenant commands and marches the first platoon as prescribed for the reserve in the forward deployment. The fifth sergeant in front of the centre of the deploying platoon, the third sergeant at its right, and second at its left. The first and fourth | | |

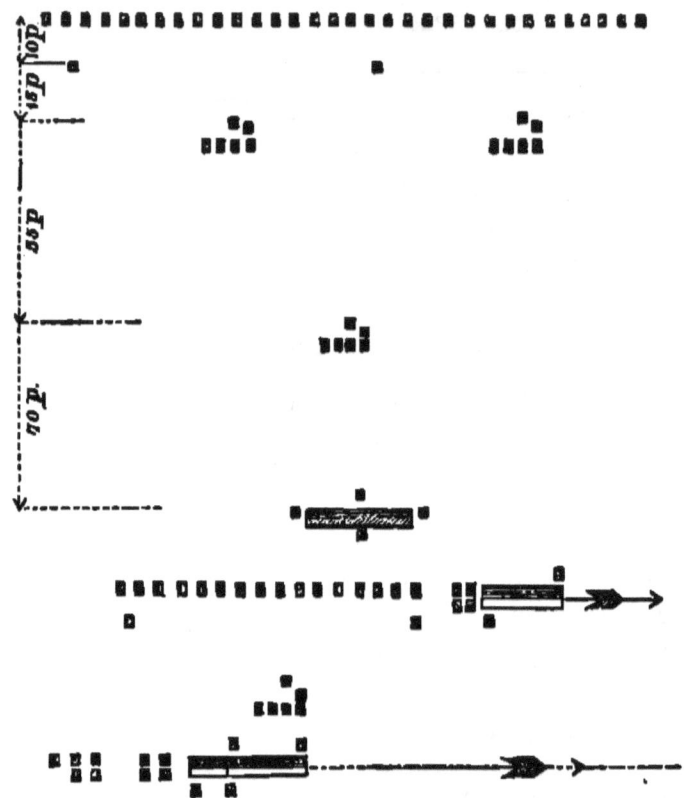

| Explanations. | Commands | |
|---|---|---|
| | Of Captain. | Of Lieutenant. |
| sergeants as guides of the reserve.......... | 2. *By the right flank, take intervals.* | |
| The first and third lieutenants take post two paces behind the left group of their sections............... | 3. MARCH (or *double-quick* MARCH). | |
| The left group stands fast, the others face to the right and move off, halt in succession as each attains the distance of twenty paces from the group in its rear, face to the front and deploy by groups, as in the forward deployment. The third sergeant on its left, conducts the right group. Chiefs of sections follow up the movement, keeping near and supervising the groups as they halt. The deployment ended, officers and | | |

| Explanations. | Commands | |
|---|---|---|
| | of Captain. | of Lieutenant. |

sergeants take the posts prescribed in the forward deployment. The first platoon, as a reserve, likewise taking its position similarly.

If the extension is to be made by the *left flank*, the command is given accordingly, the principle is the same.

To deploy by both flanks the captain will command.............. 1. *Second platoon, as skirmishers.*

All the dispositions are made as in the last deployment.......... 2. *By the right and left flanks, take intervals.*

The first lieutenant behind the left group of the third section, the third lieutenant behind the right group of the fourth section......... 3. March (or double-quick March).

The two sections (except the right group of the fourth section which stands fast) face out-

| Explanations. | Commands | |
|---|---|---|
| | of Captain. | of Lieutenant. |
| ward, and march off in opposite directions. As soon as there is the interval of twenty paces, the group that stood fast deploys, the others deploying successively as they attain their distances. The third sergeant conducts, on its left, the right file, the second sergeant the left. | | |

On the same principle the deployment may be made in any interior group, the fifth sergeant being placed before it to indicate the point. The whole company may be deployed, like the platoon.

The foregoing movements complete the deployments.

### To extend and to close intervals.

The intervals here referred to are those that separate the groups (twenty paces) and not those between the men (five paces). The principle is precisely that of the deployments, being either *forward* or *by the flank*.

The line of skirmishers being already formed, the captain wishing to separate the *groups* still further, and toward the left, upon the *same line* of battle, will command:

110   TO EXTEND AND TO CLOSE INTERVALS.

| EXPLANATIONS. | COMMANDS ||
|---|---|---|
| | OF CAPTAIN. | OF LIEUTENANT. |

1. *By the left flank (so many paces) extend intervals.* 2. MARCH (or *double-quick* MARCH.)

At the word of execution, the right group halts, or if already halted it stands fast, the others face to the left, take the new distance prescribed, then halt, facing to the front. The distance is reckoned from the nearest man of one group to the nearest of the neighboring group. Officers and sergeants supervise, lead, and finally post themselves, as in deployments by the flank. And, as in those deployments, the extension may be made by either, or by both flanks, upon any designated group. The principle is the same. If made on an interior group, the fifth sergeant* makes it.

If it be intended to make the extension of intervals, on a line in *advance* of the existing line of skirmishers, the company (or platoon being either at a halt, or in march), the captain will command............ | 1. *On the left (right, or centre) group (—— paces) extend intervals.* 2. MARCH (or *double-quick*—MARCH).

The directing group conducted by the guide, marches directly forward, the others ex-

---

* The organization not providing a fifth sergeant, commanders of skirmishing companies will find it necessary to advance a corporal to the place of *Lance* sergeant.

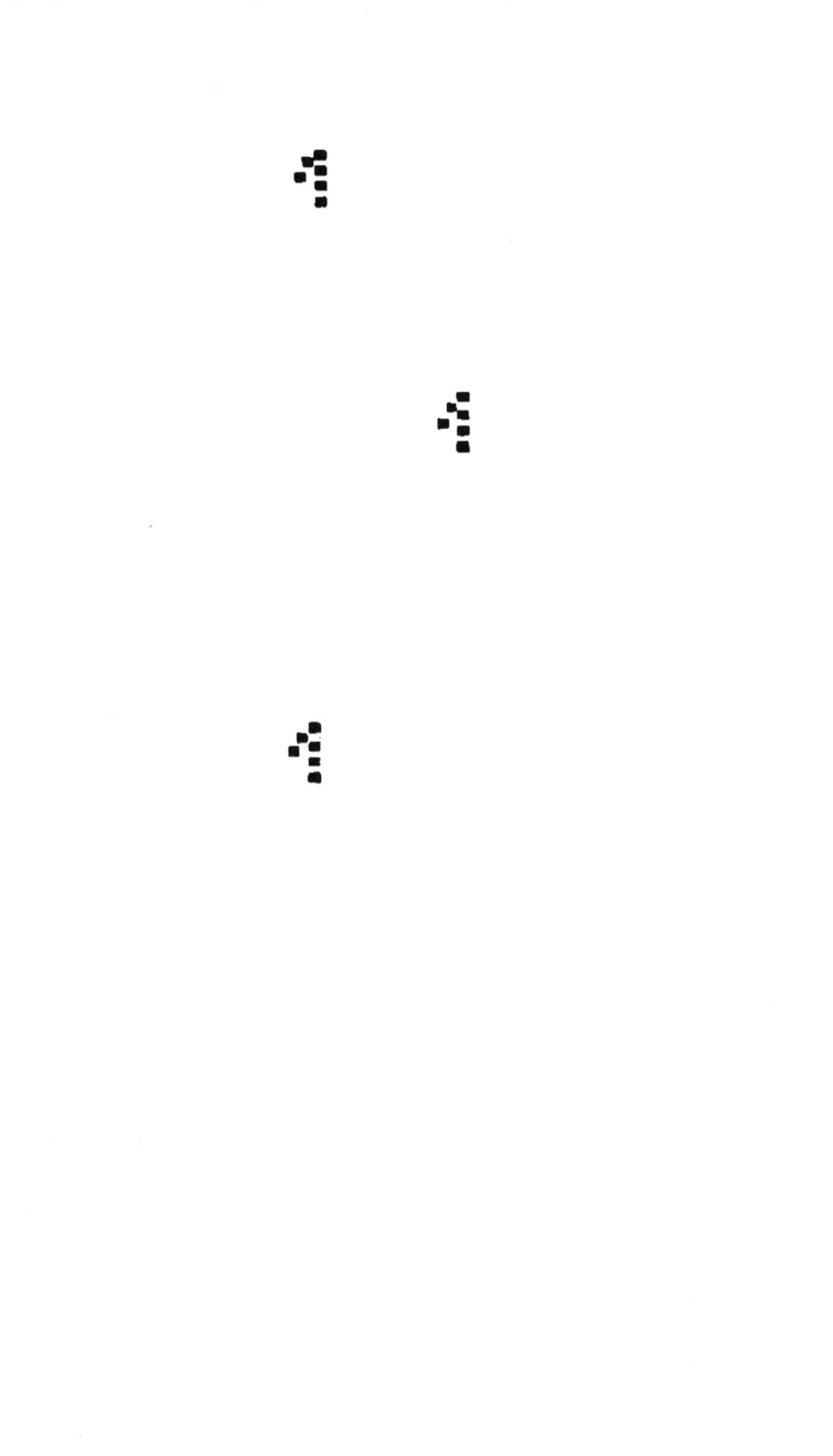

## TO CLOSE INTERVALS.

| Explanations. | Commands ||
|---|---|---|
| | Of Captain. | Of Lieutenant. |
| tend out from it, at a quicker step, gain the increased distance, and then move forward in line with the directing group. | | |

### To close intervals.

This movement is performed on the reverse principle of the extension. If the groups are to close by a flank movement, that is upon the *existing line of battle*, the captain will command.

1. *By the right* (or *left*) *flank* (— *paces*) *close intervals.*
2. MARCH, (or *double-quick—* MARCH.)

The right (or left) group standing fast, the others face to the designated flank, take the new distance, halt successively, and facing to the front.

If the closing is to be made on an interior group, the fifth sergeant marks it, as in the deployment, when the captain commands

1. *By the right and left flanks* (— *paces*) *close intervals, &c.*

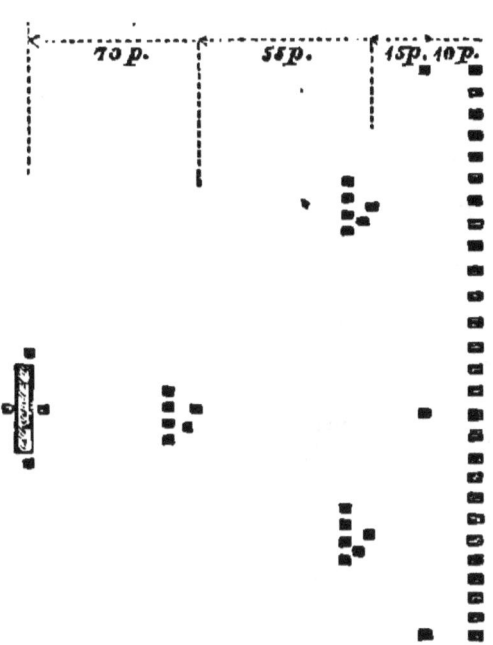

114 TO SUPPORT AND TO RELIEVE SKIRMISHERS.

| Explanations. | Commands | |
|---|---|---|
| | Of Captain. | Of Lieutenant. |
| The groups, except the one designated face inward, close upon the former, to the prescribed distance, halt, facing to the front. | | |
| If the closing is not to be made upon the existing line of skirmishers, but in *advance* of that line, the captain commands............ | 1. *On the left (right* or *centre) group (so many paces) close intervals, &c.* | |
| The directing group conducted by the guide, moves directly forward, the others inclining diagonally toward it, till the prescribed distance is attained, then moving directly to the front, dressing on the directing group. | | |

The extension and the close may be made upon any group—either by a flank or a forward movement, whether the skirmishers are faced to the front or the rear, in march, or at a halt.

### To support and to relieve skirmishers.

When the same extent of front is to be occupied by two companies, that had been held by one, the

## TO SUPPORT AND TO RELIEVE SKIRMISHERS.

| EXPLANATIONS. | COMMANDS ||
|---|---|---|
| | OF CAPTAIN. | OF LIEUTENANT. |

supporting company deploys so as to be extended at twenty paces in rear of the right or left half of the line, and the new company moves upon the line, successively, as the groups of the old company, in closing, unmask it. (So that the whole front may remain continuous and unbroken.) The reserves of the two companies, in the rear, unite.

If the line has been occupied by two companies, and one of them is now to hold the same front, that the two had held, when it extends for that purpose, the company that retires will fall to the rear, by successive files, as they are replaced by the extension.

When a company is to be relieved, the captain will be informed, who will immediately inform the chiefs of platoons. The relieving company deploys forward, halting at twenty paces in rear of the line. Its captain then marches it rapidly a few paces beyond the former line and halts it. The old line assembles on the reserve—but not forming into *groups* until beyond the enemy's fire.

If the line to be relieved is in retreat, the relieving line deploys by the flank—and the old line passing through the intervals, forms on the reserve.

The general rule of light infantry, is to hold one half the force in reserve. But, at need, the reserve may be deployed as a supporting, or as a relieving line. Both platoons should be exercised in these two movements.

## ARTICLE II.

### The movement of deployed lines.

Deployed lines may move directly to the front or rear, by either flank; may file and wheel.

They may fire at a halt or while in motion, except during the wheel.

### To advance the line.

| Explanations. | Commands of Captain. | Commands of Lieutenant. |
|---|---|---|
| The captain commands............ | 1. *Forward.* | |
| The right, left, and centre guides throw themselves on the line, at its right, left, and centre............... | 2. MARCH (or *double-quick* —MARCH). | MARCH. |
| The skirmishers step off, the guide is always at the centre, unless the command has been given *Guide right* (or *left*). Chiefs of platoon (or section) keep their places in rear. | | |
| At the command.... | HALT. | HALT. |
| Chiefs of platoons (or | | |

## TO ADVANCE THE LINE. 117

| Explanations. | Commands of Captain. | of Lieutenant. |
|---|---|---|
| sections) promptly rectify the line, and they and the guides fall back to their posts in rear. | | |

In all the *movements* of the line of skirmishers the guides are on the line, except when the firings take place. In the firings, the guides are in rear.

| | | |
|---|---|---|
| The line being in march to the front, or at a halt, the captain commands............ | 1. *In retreat.* | |
| The guides throw themselves in the line. | 2. March (or double-quick —March). | |
| The skirmishers face about, and march to the rear, *dressing* on the centre. | | |
| At the command... | Halt. | Halt. |
| The line faces about in halting, chiefs rectify it, and they and the guides fall to the rear. | | |

The line marching to the front, or to the rear, or being at a halt, the captain commands....

| | | |
|---|---|---|
| | 1. *By the right (or left) flank* | |
| The guides on the line................ | 2. March (or double-quick —March). | March. |

## TO ADVANCE THE LINE.

| EXPLANATIONS. | COMMANDS OF CAPTAIN. | OF LIEUTENANT. |
|---|---|---|
| The skirmishers face to the designated flank, and march off, the leading man conducted, on the side toward the enemy, by the guide. | | |
| At the command... | HALT. | HALT. |
| The line halts facing to the enemy. [This rule is invariable.] Guides retire. | | |
| Marching by the flank—or at a halt, the captain may cause the skirmishers to change directions by the commands, 1. *By file right* (or *left*). 2. MARCH, in the one case, and in the other, by the command, 1. *By the right flank by file left* (or *right*). 2. MARCH—and inversely. | | |
| To change front by *wheeling*, the captain commands ............... | 1. *Right* (or *left*) *wheel.* | |
| The guides on the line ................ | 2. MARCH (or *double-quick* —MARCH). | |
| The guide at the marching flank takes the full step, describing a circle, the guide at the centre takes a half step, the skirmishers | | |

| EXPLANATIONS. | COMMANDS ||
| | OF CAPTAIN. | OF LIEUTENANT. |
|---|---|---|
| proportion their steps to their distances from the guide. When the wheel is *forward*, to cease wheeling, the command is... at which the line moves directly forward. | 1. *Forward.* 2. MARCH. | MARCH. |
| If the wheel was made to the rear, the march is resumed, by the command......... At this the line ceases to wheel and marches to the rear. | 1. *In retreat.* 2. MARCH. | MARCH. |

In the foregoing cases, at the command HALT—the line halts, facing to the front, if the wheel was made toward the rear.

If the line is advancing, or at a halt, in order to throw back a flank to the rear, the commands are, 1. *In retreat.* 2. MARCH, followed by 1. *Right* (or *left*) *wheel*—MARCH.

The reserve is held in rear of the centre, and follows the movements of the line. At the command *Halt*, like the line, it faces to the enemy, without a further command. To march it forward its chief commands, 1. *Platoon, forward.* 2. *Guide left.* 3. MARCH. To march to the rear—1. *In retreat.* 2. MARCH. 3. *Guide right.*

*Forward* means toward the enemy; *in retreat*

| Explanations. | Commands ||
|---|---|---|
| | of Captain. | of Lieutenant. |

means to retire, and *right* and *left flank* refer to the flank which is then, whatever the position, at the right or left. Thus, if marching by a flank, the command, to move to the front is, 1. *Forward.* 2. MARCH—to move to the rear, 1. *In retreat.* 2. MARCH.

## ARTICLE III.

### The firings.

Whether the fire of skirmishers is commenced from a halt, or while marching to the front, rear, or by either flank, the captain commands.... | *Commence firing.* | *Commence firing.*
To stop the fire the captain commands.... | *Cease firing.* | *Cease firing.*

Both these commands are promptly repeated by the lieutenants and sergeants.

Being at a halt, at the command *Commence firing* the front-rank men fire (but not all at the same time), the rear rank men reserve their fire till their respective front-rank has loaded—when they likewise fire—the ranks alternating thus till the command is recalled.

### To fire marching to the front.

The command *Commence firing* is given and repeated. The front-rank men halt, fire and re-

| Explanations. | Commands | |
|---|---|---|
| | Of Captain. | Of Lieutenant. |

load. The rear-rank men of their files continue to march, halt at eight or ten paces, beyond their front-rank men, and fire when the latter have loaded. The fire is thus alternated between the front and rear rank men. If the command *halt* is given, the line is formed forward, on the *advanced* skirmishers.

### To fire marching in retreat.

At the unvarying command, the front-rank men halt, fire—and throw themselves to the rear, loading—the rear-rank men marching ten or twelve paces beyond the former, halt, face about, and fire, after the front-rank men have passed ten or twelve paces, have halted and reloaded. The fire is so continued. If *halt* is commanded, the line forms on the skirmishers who are *in rear*.

### To fire marching by the flank.

If the command is given when marching by the *right* flank, the front-rank man, of each file, faces to the enemy, steps a pace to the front and fires, while his rear-rank man marches on. Having fired, the front-rank man, loading on the march, follows the rear-rank man, who steps out, when the other has loaded, fires and follows in his turn. The files must not intermix, and when *Cease* FIRING is commanded, the front and rear rank man, if not in their original places, resume them.

| Explanations. | Commands | |
|---|---|---|
| | of Captain. | of Lieutenant. |

If the march be by the left flank, it is the men of the *rear* rank who commence the fire. The method of alternation then continues as before.

If the fire is from a halt, and the command is given, 1. *Forward*—MARCH, the men whose pieces are loaded, advance, the others finish loading, and the fire proceeds as in the usual fire when marching by the front. If the skirmishers are firing *in march by the flank*, the same rule is observed—the men whose pieces are loaded stepping out to fire.

On the contrary, if the line is firing from a halt, whilst advancing, or when marching by a flank, and the command is given, *In retreat*—MARCH, the men whose pieces are loaded remain in line, the others throw themselves to the rear loading, and the usual fire alternates as in the case of firing in retreat.

If the line is firing advancing, retiring, or at a halt, at the command, *By the right* (or *left*) *flank* —MARCH, it is the men who have their pieces loaded that step out toward the enemy and deliver the fire, their fellows of the same file continuing the march.

[The purpose of all these arrangements is, obviously, to oppose the enemy with the loaded and not the unloaded pieces.

It will be observed that the principle of the firings is based upon *files*, while that of the deployments rests upon *groups*.]

## ARTICLE IV.

### The rallies,

May be made by groups of fours, by sections, by platoons, or on the reserve.

Preparatory to rallying, the command, or signal, is given to *fix bayonets*.

| Explanations. | Commands of Captain. | Commands of Lieutenant. |
|---|---|---|
| The company in march, or at a halt, the captain commands .......... Officers and sergeants repeat the command. If in march, the line halts. Each group forms a little square of four, facing outward on the even-numbered front-rank man, who takes the position of *guard against cavalry;*\* facing *forward*, his rear-rank man forms on his left, the odd front-rank on his right, and odd rear-rank man on his rear. The right feet of the men (all *guard-* | *Rally by fours.* | *Rally by fours* |

---

\* See Bayonet Fencing.

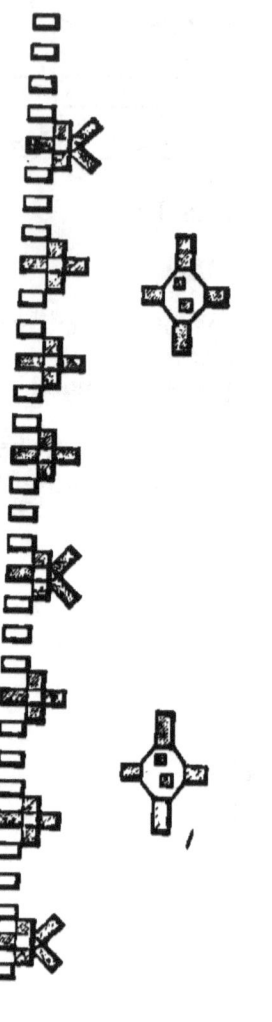

## TO RALLY BY SECTIONS.

| EXPLANATIONS. | COMMANDS | |
|---|---|---|
| | OF CAPTAIN. | OF LIEUTENANT. |
| *ing against cavalry*) form a square. They load and fire without moving the feet. The captain and lieutenants, with their buglers, place themselves within the squares formed by their groups, the sergeants within the nearest groups of the line. | | |
| To re-form the line the captain commands, | *Deploy as skirmishers.* | |
| which is executed as in the deployments. | | |

NOTE. The rallies are all made at the *run*, which is two hundred steps, of thirty-three inches, to the minute. If the bayonets have not been *fixed*, the skirmishers fix bayonets, whilst rallying.

### To rally by sections.

| | | |
|---|---|---|
| The skirmishing being in line, the captain commands............... | *Rally by sections.* | *Rally by sections.* |
| Chiefs of sections throw themselves into the square, formed by one of the *interior* groups | | |

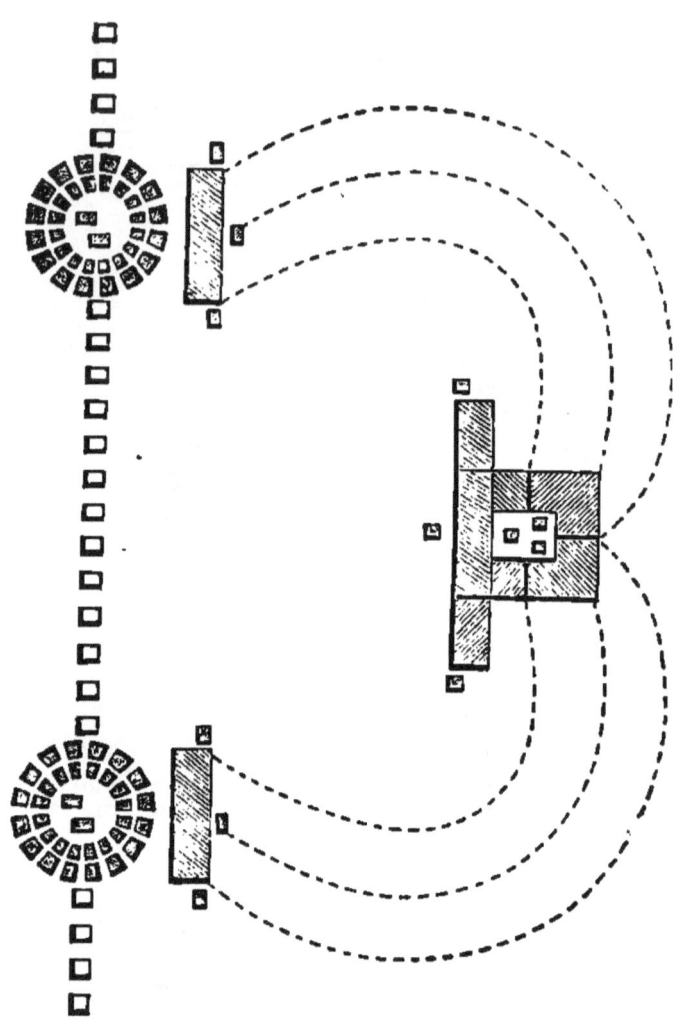

| Explanations. | Commands ||
|---|---|---|
| | of Captain. | of Lieutenant. |
| they may select for the points of the rally. This group throws up the points of its bayonets, as a sign to the others, which form rapidly around it, filling up its angles, and making a circle of the entire section. The men as they form, come to a *charge bayonets* (points more elevated) and cock their pieces. The two outer ranks fire and load without moving their feet. | | |
| To deploy the circles the captain commands, | *Form sections.* | *Form sections* |
| The chiefs dress the sections on the files that are facing the enemy, the men taking their numbered places. | | |

## Rally by platoons.

This rally is made on the same principle as the last, and the circle is deployed in the same way.

In both the foregoing rallies, the reserve also, if threatened, forms a circle around its chief.

| Explanations. | Commands ||
|---|---|---|
| | OF CAPTAIN. | OF LIEUTENANT. |

**Rally on the reserve.**

At this command the reserve forms half of a square, by throwing back its flank half sections, the men come to the *ready*, and open their fire as soon as the reserve is unmasked by the skirmishers. The latter form into groups upon the man of the group who is nearest the centre of the section. The groups incline to each other so as to form into sections; these are so directed by their chiefs, to the right and left, as to unmask the reserve, arrived at which they complete the square, and join in its fire, without waiting for a command.

If, during its march on the reserve, the chief of section command *Halt*, the section immediately forms circle around the officer.

| Explanations. | Commands | |
|---|---|---|
| | Of Captain. | Of Lieutenant. |

If the whole company is deployed, and the command is given *Rally on the battalion*, the skirmishers direct themselves toward the nearest flank, and having passed its file-closers, form, in quick time ten paces in their rear. If there are several platoons so formed in rear of the battalion wings, they will be in close column, or at half-distance.

If the battalion is in square, the rallying skirmishers enter by its rear angles, and form close column of platoons in rear of its first front. If the battalion is in column *to form square*, the skirmishers form similarly in rear of the centre of the third division, and march forward, closing on the buglers, at the command *Form square*—MARCH.

If the square is formed, and cannot be safely opened, the skirmishers will throw themselves at the feet of the front rank, dropping on the right knee, butt on the thigh, and bayonet advanced. They will, in the same way occupy the sectors without fire (the angles).

Skirmishers rallied behind the wings of the battalion, will be marched by the flank, through the interval (between battalions) when they are again to deploy in front of the battalion. In the case of their having been rallied in the interior of a column or square, they will be marched out by the flank and deployed again, as prescribed for the deployment of platoons at half-distance.

| EXPLANATIONS. | COMMANDS | |
|---|---|---|
| | OF CAPTAIN. | OF LIEUTENANT. |

### Skirmishers in square and column.

The skirmishers having *rallied on the reserve*, and formed square under the immediate direction of the captain, he will hold it either in square, or in column at half distance, by platoon.

| | | |
|---|---|---|
| The captain commands............ | 1. *Form column.* <br> 2. MARCH. | |
| The guides place themselves on the right and left of the platoons, those of the second at half distance from the rear-rank of the first platoon, the platoons dress on their centres, the rear platoon facing about. | | |
| To form square again the captain commands, | 1. *Form square* <br> 2. MARCH. | |
| If in march the column halts, the platoon in rear faces about, both platoons throw back their flank half sections, forming the square as at first. | | |

SKIRMISHERS IN SQUARE AND COLUMN. 131

| EXPLANATIONS. | COMMANDS | |
|---|---|---|
| | OF CAPTAIN. | OF LIEUTENANT. |
| If the column is to march in advance, the captain commands.... | 1. *Forward.* 2. MARCH (or *double-quick* —MARCH). | |
| The column steps off and the captain adds, | 3. *Guide left* (or *right*). | |
| The men touch toward the guide. To march in retreat. The company faces about, and marches in the opposite direction. The captain adding... | 1. *In retreat.* 2. MARCH (or *double-quick* —MARCH). 3. *Guide right* (or *left*). | |

The *column* will be preserved; if it is to move toward either flank, this will be done by *wheeling*, (not by *turning*, or by the flank march).

Being in column the first platoon may be deployed as already explained. To deploy the second, the captain commands............. | 1. *Second platoon as skirmishers.*

The chief of the first platoon cautions it to stand fast, chiefs of sections in the second place themselves before their centres. The

132 SKIRMISHERS IN SQUARE AND COLUMN.

| Explanations. | Commands | |
| --- | --- | --- |
| | of Captain. | of Lieutenant. |
| fifth sergeant a pace in front of the centre of the second platoon.... | 2. *On the centre file—take intervals.* | |
| The chief of the third section adds.... | ............ | Section right face. |
| Chief of the fourth section............... | ............ | Section left face. |
| The captain then commands............... | 3. March. | |
| The sections march off, the fifth sergeant with the fourth section. When each passes the flank of the first platoon, its chief commands............... | ............ | By the left flank—March (or By the right flank—March). |
| and the moment the sections are on the alignment of the first platoon both chiefs command............... | ............ | As skirmishers—March. |
| The groups deploy forward on the fifth | | |

## THE ASSEMBLY.

| Explanations. | Commands ||
|---|---|---|
| | Of Captain. | Of Lieutenant. |
| sergeant, who conducts the right group of the fourth section. | | |

If the deployment is to be by the flank, the only difference is that the sections pass the first platoon several paces, are then halted, and deployed by the flank.

### The assembly,

Is intended simply to annul the deployment. While the rallies are always made at the *run*, the assemblies are made in the *quick* step.

The line being deployed, and at a halt, the captain commands: *Assemble by the right* (or *left*) *flank*. The skirmishers face to the designated flank—close toward its last group, which is forming itself, the other groups form in marching, close up successively, face to the front, and support arms.

To assemble by both flanks, the command is varied accordingly, the skirmishers face inward, and close upon the designated group.

| | | |
|---|---|---|
| To assemble while marching to the front, the captain, if he wish the formation to be on the centre, which would be the shortest way, commands............. | *Assemble on the centre.* | |
| The centre guide marches directly on, followed by the direct- | | |

| Explanations. | Commands | |
|---|---|---|
| | of Captain. | of Lieutenant. |

ing file toward which the other comrades of that group incline. The men of the other groups form into groups upon those of their files nearest the directing file; the groups being formed incline toward, and successively unite with, the centre group, and bring their pieces to the right shoulder.

The step of the inclining files and groups is necessarily *quickened*.

The assembly may be made on the right, left or any other file. A guide should conduct the file. A line marching in retreat, is assembled on the same principle—the front-rank men following their rear-rank men.

### Assemble on the reserve.

At this command the skirmishers reform the groups, on the line, the groups direct themselves upon the reserve, the rear rank leading, form themselves upon it in their proper places, and faced to the front. The company joins the battalion.

| Explanations. | Commands ||
|---|---|---|
| | of Captain. | of Lieutenant. |

## Manœuvres of Skirmishers.

The manœuvres of skirmishers consist in great measure of the movements of single companies, but the same principles are readily applicable to a battalion.

The battalion may be deployed as skirmishers, either from line of battle or from close column of companies.

The colonel designates in advance the companies that are to constitute the reserve, under the major. They are taken from the right or left flank, when the battalion is in line, and from the rear when it is in close column.

Each company (or platoon) covers, when deployed, a front of one hundred paces.

Whether the deployment is made from line, or from column, the words of command by the colonel are the same: the words of command of the captains, in deploying their companies (or platoons) are those of the company drill.

For the movements of the line when deployed—extending, closing intervals, the firings, &c.—the colonel applies the commands of the company drill, and the principle of the execution is absolutely the same.

A battalion of eight companies, being in line of battle, to hold in reserve the first, second, and third companies, and to deploy forward the remaining five on the right of the sixth, the colonel will make

| Explanations. | Commands | |
|---|---|---|
| | of Captain. | of Lieutenant. |

known his intention to the lieutenant-colonel, major, and adjutant—directing the major to take charge of the reserve, and instructing the lieutenant-colonel as to the proposed direction of the line, and as to the point where the right of the sixth company is to rest. The lieutenant-colonel throws himself eight or ten paces in front of the sixth company's right, the adjutant the same distance in front of its left, the major in front of the intended reserve.

| Explanations. | of Captain. | of Lieutenant. |
|---|---|---|
| The colonel then commands............. | 1. *First* (or *second*) *platoons, as skirmishers.* 2. *On the right of the sixth company—take intervals.* | |
| The captain of the sixth company prepares to deploy his first platoon on its right file. The captain of the fifth to deploy his first platoon on its left file. The captain of the fourth company commands................. | ............ | *Right face.* |
| Captains of the seventh and eighth companies.. | ............ | *Left face.* |
| The colonel adds... | March (or *double-quick*—March). | March. |

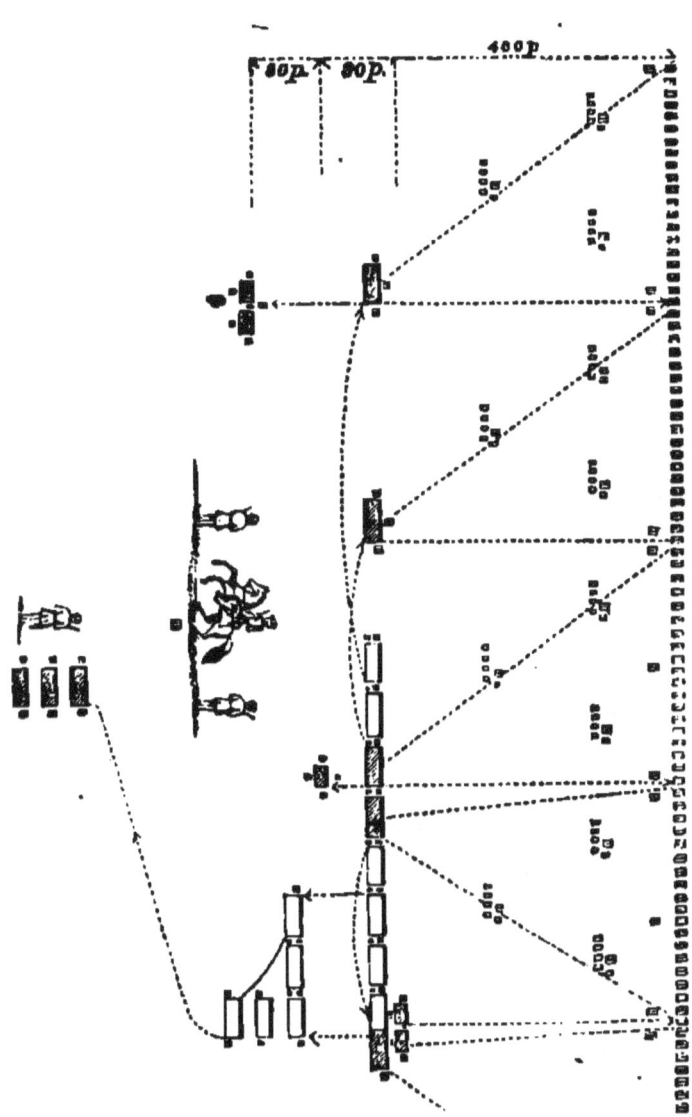

| Explanations. | Commands | |
|---|---|---|
| | Of Captain. | Of Lieutenant. |
| The platoons of the fifth and sixth companies deploy forward. The fourth company, marching by its right flank, halts when opposite the right flank (deployed) of the fifth company, faces then to the front, deploys forward its first platoon on the left file, throwing its reserve to the rear. The seventh and eighth companies gain distance to the left flank in the same manner, halt successively, and deploy in the same manner on their right files. The companies deployed dress on the directing company (in this instance the sixth). | | |

The lieutenant-colonel and adjutant follow up the deployment on the right and left respectively, and afterward place themselves in rear and near the colonel, posted two hundred paces in rear.

The major, on an order from the colonel, will have faced about and marched the three right

| Explanations. | Commands ||
| | of Captain. | of Lieutenant. |

companies directly to the rear thirty paces. halted, ployed into column at half distance, and afterwards he will have marched this battalion reserve to occupy the point selected for it by the colonel.

The company reserves are posted in *echelon*, descending from the right to the left (or, it may be, from left to right). The reserves of two companies are united, to form a stronger resistance to cavalry. In the present instance, the several reserves are posted—that of the sixth company, one hundred and fifty paces in rear of its right: the reserves of the fourth and fifth companies in rear of the centre of their line thirty paces in advance of that of the sixth, and the reserve of the seventh and eighth companies, opposite the centre of their line, thirty paces to the rear of the reserve of the sixth company. Thus, in an even number of deployed companies, the reserves would be half the number of the companies.

The battalion being in line of battle to deploy the companies *by the flank*, instead of deploying them *forward*—on the same point of direction—that is, on the right of the sixth company—the colonel commands as before—the captains of the sixth and fifth companies march them ten or twelve paces forward, by the commands: 1. *Forward*. 2. *Guide* RIGHT. 3. MARCH. They halt their companies and deploy them by the flank—the sixth by the left, the fifth by the right flank, as in the company drill—the reserve, if *platoons* are deployed, being

| Explanations. | Commands | |
|---|---|---|
| | OF CAPTAIN. | OF LIEUTENANT. |

marched to the rear. The other companies march by the flank—those to the right of the directing companies by the right flank, the others by the left—halt when their distance of one hundred paces is attained—move forward on the line, and deploy by the flank. Each will wait till the next platoon toward the side of direction shall have finished its deployment.

### Deployment of Skirmishers from Column.

The *close* column must be first formed.

Whether this deployment be made forward or by the flank, the directing company is moved forward ten or twelve paces in advance of the position just occupied by the head of the column. It is then deployed as commanded. The other companies march to their proper distance, to the right or left with respect to the directing company, then deploy individually, as before, whether forward or by the flank. (The deployment of skirmishers from column is the combination of *deploying into line of battle* and this line's *extension into skirmishing order*.)

When the color company is one of those to be deployed, the guard remains with the company, the color is detached to the battalion reserve.

When *Assemble on the battalion* is sounded, the companies assemble on their reserves, and then join the battalion reserve, taking their proper places in column.

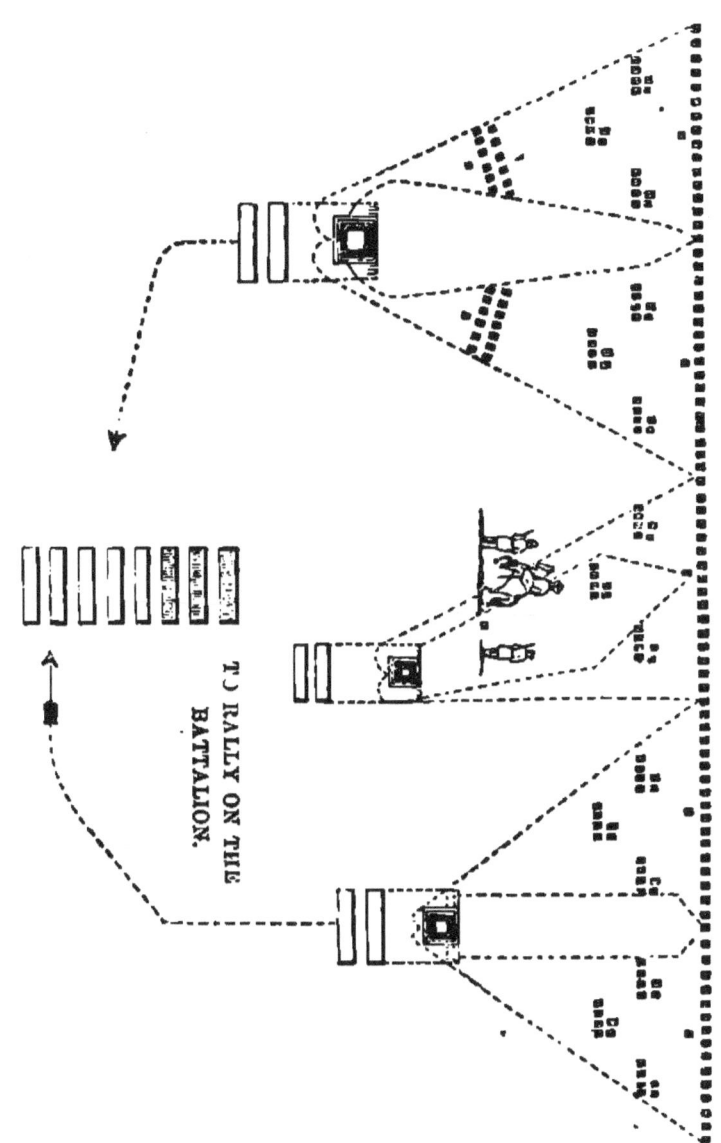

TO RALLY ON THE BATTALION.

| Explanations. | Commands | |
|---|---|---|
| | Of Captain. | Of Lieutenant. |

### Rallies.

All the rallies may be performed as prescribed for the company.

When *Rally on the battalion* is sounded, the skirmishers unite with their company reserves to form square—the reserve throwing back its flank sections, and the skirmishers continuing the formation, the last who run in completing the rear front—facing outward, in two ranks, and without regard to height.

These squares march upon the battalion reserve (forming themselves into column) as soon as they are able, or they seize any advantageous positions, in the interim.

The battalion reserve, if threatened by cavalry, forms square.

The colonel disposes the battalion reserve to protect the rally.

If the battalion reserve be formed in square, the other reserves, in marching upon it, will take the line of its diagonals prolonged, in order to be within its sectors without fire.

If the battalion reserve be held in column, the approaching company reserves will form in column with it; not, as in *assembling*, necessarily in their regular order, but in the order of their arrival, without regard to number, next in rear of companies already in the column.

# SUPPLEMENT.

SKIRMISHERS should be *gradually* inured to the fatigue of the double-quick march, at the fixed rate of 165 steps to the minute. In this practice, it is even unsafe to continue it long in the beginning. The *run* (*pas de course*), of two hundred steps to the minute, should next be performed. Both these steps should be persistently *timed*, and their cadence well established. Without attempting here explanations of the causes, it is undeniable that rhythmic movements are performed with much less of exhaustion to the human frame, than unregulated efforts, and especially is this the fact when a consentaneous action of masses is required.

The French tactics (and their translators) err somewhat in saying that the double-quick step differs from the quick step only in its greater rate of march. In the *walk*, however fast, there is no instant during which both the feet are off the ground; while in the *run*, however slowly performed, there is, during each propulsion, a perceptible space when neither foot is in contact with the earth. The eye detects the difference easily. The double-quick (*pas gymnastique*), is in fact a slow run (or *trot*), and there probably never has been a time when this pace was not actually used in war. The step should be taken lightly, the weight falling on the ball of the foot, the knees somewhat bent, but the legs flexible (not rigid), while the trunk should be kept as steady and immovable as possible. The arms should be contracted, because the bracing of the arm, shoulder, and pectoral muscles conduces to the strength and steadiness of the chest. The inspirations should be made quickly and deeply, and the expirations very slowly. The body more and more leaned *forward* as the march is prolonged. To be able to sustain the exertion required, the step must be practised and performed on right principles.

It is quite apparent that when the directing portion of a line is in quick time, and is to move over a shorter distance, that part that is to conform to it, and to traverse a greater distance, must move more rapidly. If, therefore, the time is commanded *quick*, *all* but the directing fraction, are to take double-quick time; and if *double-quick* is commanded, these latter must take the run. *Quick* time, then, is rather the exception than the rule in the skirmishers' drill.

Skirmishers are to carry their arms substantially "at will," but the *trail* (in either of the hands), has such advantages as these: it allows the soldier to drop upon the ground or under cover readily; to climb a fence, or cross a ditch or stream; fix his bayonet; and does not so much expose him to be seen, as when the piece is carried at or upon the shoulder.

Skirmishers must know how to take advantage of the ground, of knolls, trees, rocks, fences, walls, &c. When a group gets possession of such cover, the comrades are to give place to one another to fire from it. The passage from one cover to another must be made warily, taking care to load before quitting the former place.

Skirmishers are to be exercised in loading and firing while kneeling, sitting, or lying on the ground, taking care that in loading the piece is held upright (the butt may be tapped on the ground), for an instant, before ramming.

It is quite important that practice at the long ranges be made—the efficiency of light infantry depending much on the individual fire—marksmanship is a necessary part of the instruction. The alternation of the fire, between the front and rear rank men, must yield to its deliberation and effectiveness, as the precision of the alignment must not interfere with the cover to the skirmishers afforded by the circumstances of the ground. The non-commissioned officers will see that the men get under cover when practicable, and that they do not fire without deliberate aim—not rapidly but with effect. It is more than ordinarily important in skirmishing, to husband the ammunition.

It has been seen that skirmishers load before they advance, and in retiring, fall back immediately after firing—to leave the front clear and to avoid needless exposure.

Should skirmishers be *dispersed*, by an over-sudden attack, the men must shift for themselves, take trees, get up banks, behind fences, resort to the bayonet fencing, and fire at any opportunity. The officers must get together a few files, and endeavor to effect a rally upon some good positions In the case of a detached company, it is advisable, to provide for such a casualty, by appointing beforehand some general place of rendezvous. There are noted instances where light troops have been so reassembled, without suffering great loss, after having been driven back and scattered.

Artillery has little effect upon the extended line of skirmishers, especially if they are lying flat on the ground or well covered—while their fire falls in return with great effect upon the other. In firing upon a battery the flanks of the line should endeavor to close forward, to obtain the advantage of the cross-fire, and the horses in rear should be selected as an object in order to disable the pieces for retreating. Moving the line thirty or forty paces forward, or to the rear, after the artillery has gotten its range, will serve to disconcert it.

When light infantry support artillery they should, usually, be posted on one or both flanks (not yet deployed, it may be), and a part of them may find a position from which to cross their fire with that of the artillery; if the guns advance, the light infantry may be ordered to cover their front, or to move forward parallel with them. In retiring, the infantry skirmishes to cover the withdrawal of the guns, and to afford them time to gain some distance to the rear.

In a broken or intersected country, and in woody and soft meadow lands, light infantry have the advantage over cavalry. In such ground cavalry will not venture to engage, seriously, skirmishers who manifest a resolute opposition. A single infantry man, who knows the use of his bayonet, is at least a match for an individual horseman.

Forty paces between groups is the extreme interval of deployment. The habitual distance being twenty paces, if a less distance be named in the command, the men in the groups must reduce their intervals to correspond.

In covering the front of a battalion (in line), the skirmishers must extend beyond the battalion front half the interval to the next battalions on its right, and left.

Whether covering the front of the battalion, or its flank, and whether the battalion be in column or line, the skirmishers are to conform their movements to it.

Should it be in line, and a flank unsupported, skirmishers are either to be extended along the flank, or to be so far extended along the front as to protect the flank.

If the battalion moves in *echelon*, the skirmishers must half face, and gain ground, in the proper direction by obliquing.

If the battalion passes into column from line, the skirmishers will preserve their extension to cover the movement. If they are masking the head of a column, they will be extended so far as to cover the deployment of the column into line.

When the formation in rear of the skirmishers is complete, and they are ordered to quit the front, they must leave it clear as soon as possible.

They should not cross the *front* of a square or of a column.

Skirmishers should be thrown forward to cover a change of front of the battalion.

If covering a line that moves to the attack, skirmishers should be closed, at the proper moment, to the right and left to clear the front.

But it frequently happens that the skirmishers,

in the enemy's attack upon troops in position, are driven directly back upon them. In this case the troops of the line should throw back a few files from the left of the companies, opening intervals for the skirmishers to pass through.

When a line of skirmishers, whether advancing or retreating, is halted, they should lose no time in availing themselves of the cover the ground may afford. The non-commissioned officers should look to this.

If assailed by cavalry. and skirmishers can avail themselves of such an obstacle as a house, fence, or the edge of a ravine, they need not form square. Forming line with their backs to the obstacle will be sufficient.

The fatiguing nature of the duty requires that skirmishers be relieved from time to time.

### Rallies.

The essentially new part of the drill of skirmishers, is the development upon the groups of fours. In the system that prevailed anterior to this late introduction of the French, the deployment was made upon the *file* as the fundamental unit, the directing file moved forward or it stood fast, according as the deployment was to be forward or by the flank; and at the proper time the file (as now the group) deployed, the rear-rank man stopping upon the general line two paces on the left of his file leader. In extending or in closing intervals the distance taken was that between files, the distance between the men of a file remaining invariably two paces. This method certainly has simplicity in its favor. The officer in command expressed the number of paces to be taken for intervals, and was not limited, except by his discretion. In deploying by the flank, it was the duty of the front-rank man of the file to look to the direction (to follow exactly the trace of the preceding file); while the rear-rank man, casting a glance over the shoulder, determined the distance from the halting file in rear, and then cautioned his file leader, in a low tone, by the word *halt*. This, it would be well to continue with the groups.

It seems to be doubtful whether the system of groups be a positive improvement. A circumstance that strengthens the doubt is, the fact that the whole of the *firing* comes back to repose upon the *file* development. Perhaps rather too much importance is attached to the ingenious idea of the squares which are formed by the groups of fours. To calculate their value it should be considered, 1st. That any casualties that may have occurred before the formation would have rendered the numbering off erroneous, and would have made the groups less than four. The fragments would then, of course, join themselves to the neighboring squares, in which case these would no longer be *squares of four*. 2d. The smallness of the squares makes them weak in themselves. 3d. They are not formed in *echelon*, or so that their fire crosses missing one another. Other points might be reckoned going to indicate that the principle of these little squares may have been overvalued at the expense of the general theory of the skirmishing drill. However, as I have no disposition to deny the system of the groups of fours a certain merit, I limit the direct objection to the

13*

following point. Let it be granted that the aggregating of the extended group into a prompt square of fours, back to back, furnishes a ready means of strengthening the line, yet I certainly believe that the subordinating of the next higher units, that is to say, the *rally of the section and platoon circles*, to the group square is a vice. It is pushing the spirit of system too far.* The small square of four is an unsuitable nucleus for the section or platoon circle. I give the reasons: 1st. Because the formation of the circle ought to allow (and the text requires) a fire by two ranks, which are inconveniently formed on the square nucleus. 2d. Because the sergeants are thrown into the ranks, not being able to get within the nucleus, and thus are prevented from assisting the officer effectually. 3d. Because the men, running in on either flank, cannot find their proper places in front and rear of the line (of battle) while those who are already formed cannot charge bayonets promptly, on account of the continued arrival of the men from the extremes of the late line.

I propose that the section (or platoon) circle be rallied thus: The men shall run to the officer, instead of his running to them. At the command of the captain the lieutenant forms his escort (if he have one) as a segment of the inner circle, and faced toward the approaching cavalry—he throwing up his sword, and they their bayonets, for a

---

* The figure in the Tactics does not follow the text. The figure makes the circle tangent to the line of battle. The text places its centre upon the line. Hardee and Casey follow the French plate in this oversight.

signal. The first arriving files rapidly complete this first circle, the sergeants and the bugler throwing themselves into it. The men coming in later form an outer concentric circle—the whole being finally in two ranks, and the circle compact, by reason of the two facts that there are several combatants in the centre, and that the officer by disposing the segment of the first or inner circle, can determine the dimension of both the circles, and graduate it to contain accurately his section or platoon.

In forming the circle as above, the men may all take the *run* without impeding one another—they are gaining ground toward the reserve—the point of the rally is known at once, and no time is lost in the officer's passing forward to a particular group; the circle is better formed for firing. It is obvious that the officer can choose the rear of any part of his line for the formation, by simply throwing himself to the desired point.

### Flank Deployments, &c.

In the flank deployments, and in extending and closing, by the flank, it will, perhaps, be admitted on fair consideration that the men should face toward the designated point, at the command which indicates to them which it is, not delaying to face till the word MARCH. In close order, men cannot face and step off in the double-quick step, at one and the same time; they are not required to step off from a halt, by the flank, in any instance but this, which is an alteration of the drill as prescribed in Scott's tactics. At the command, *By the* ——

*flank take intervals*, the skirmishers should face preparatory to marching at the word MARCH.

The text of General Casey furnishes a means of re-forming the line, after rallying by fours, by sections and by platoons, but does not go beyond this. All rallies are made in the anticipation of ultimately gaining the reserve; and when rallied by *fours*, *sections*, or *platoons*, at the *assemble*, *rally on the reserve*, or *rally on the battalion*, the squares or circles should break up at once, and direct themselves to the rear.

In some systems of skirmishing the flanks of the deployed line are bent slightly to the rear, a few files thrown back, forming a curved line. This is, in effect, an application, on a small scale, of the principle of the *echelon*, and is a guard against being readily outflanked. There are times when its adoption would prove advantageous.

### Changes of Front.

The prescribed system does not seem to provide adequately against an attack on the flank, where it is chiefly to be apprehended. If the enemy should appear suddenly on either flank, neither *wheeling* nor *filing* would be a sufficiently prompt movement to oppose him. If the whole line is required to change front to a flank, much time would be lost, the fire would be delayed, and the outward men much fatigued.

The centre is always the point of direction, unless otherwise ordered, and upon the centre as a pivot, changes of front can best be executed in an extended line.

## SUPPLEMENT. 153

The following method is taken from systems antecedent to our present one, and seems to deserve to be adopted.

The captain wishing to change front to the right, will command, 1. *Change front to the right.* The centre guide places himself on the line, to mark the centre, the right platoon (or section) faces *about* and then half faces to the right. The left platoon (or section) half faces to the right.

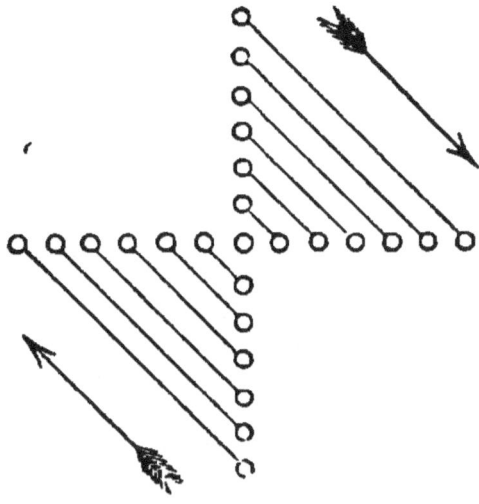

The captain commands, 2. MARCH (or *Double-quick*—MARCH). The skirmishers direct themselves, each by the shortest line, upon the new direction, arriving successively, the right wing facing about and aligning on the guide and centre group.

To change front to the left the commands and means are inverse.

If the captain wishes to change front, not on the centre, but on the extreme right or left file, the shortest way to form the new front seems to be as follows: The captain commands, 1. *Right section forward into line—left section rally*. The skirmishers of the right wing half face to the right, the guide marks the centre, those of the left wing face to the right. The reserve wheels to the right. 2. MARCH (or. *Double-quick*—MARCH). The skirmishers of the right section form successively into line on the left of the right guide, and perpendicularly to their old line; the reserve deploys forward on its left file, and upon the line of the first platoon (or section). The left platoon or section rallies in rear of the centre of the line, and acts, for the time, as its reserve.

To form line to the left, the commands and means are inverse.

This movement places fresh skirmishers in action, and one-fourth more of them on the line; a decided advantage in the case of a sudden attack.

### Flankers.

Flankers are thrown out, to prevent a sudden attack on a flank, which on a march is the most dangerous of all attacks. They must be at a sufficient distance to allow time to the column to form. The distance varies, with the country, and the kind of troops opposed. Three to four hundred paces is an ordinary distance. At night, or in foggy weather, or in a close or intersected country, or if the enemy's cavalry hover on the flanks, half the foregoing distance may suffice.

The men of a file should keep together and act in concert, one stepping out of the line to examine any suspicious place, whilst the other preserves the chain.

A company of a battalion ordered to cover both its flanks, will march out of the column, the first platoon by the right flank, the second by the left; gain two hundred paces to either flank, and deploy. The groups may be held together, or may deploy into single file. The figure p.156 will serve to represent the movement ended.

Flankers encountering any impassable impediments—streams, bogs, &c.—will not pass around them, leaving them to intervene between themselves and the column, but will close in toward the flank.

On discovering the enemy they will *instantly fire.* They will resist an attack firmly, retiring only when recalled or overpowered.

Flankers must look out for the enemy on the side they protect, should climb the elevations, and examine all places that might serve for concealment.

When the column halts, flankers should face outward, and throw out a few files as sentries.

Troops should never venture into a wood, pass, or defile, without throwing forward skirmishers, and sending out flankers.

### Advanced Guard.

The advanced guard of infantry may or may not

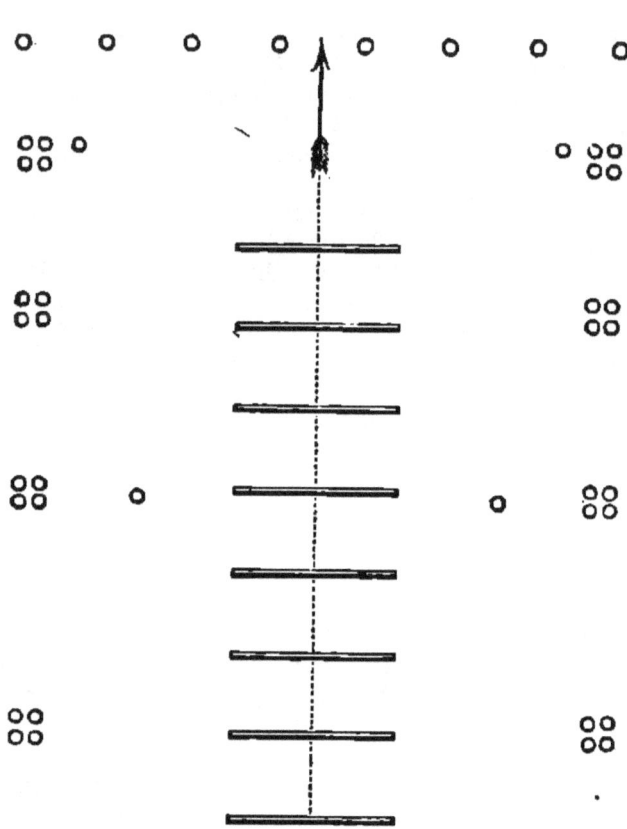

COMPANY DEPLOYED AS FLANKERS TO A COLUMN.

be deployed in skirmishing order, according to circumstances. If deployed their duties are in many respects the same as those of the flankers.

It is their duty to examine all villages, detached houses, enclosures, &c., before the near approach of the column.

If feeling for the enemy, upon discovering him they will not fire, but halt, observing his position, strength, and movements, and communicate to the rear. If, however, they are assailed, they must fire, to give instant notice, and must dispute the ground. But it must be impressed upon the men that they are not to fire unless they are perceived by the enemy, as by doing so they discover to him the presence of their own army.

### Rear Guard.

Light infantry in the rear guard, may be undeployed, or it may be in skirmishing order, according to circumstances. If the column be advancing, the infantry of the rear guard is not usually deployed. But if the column be retreating before an enemy, the light infantry is formed in skirmishing order. Their proper front is toward the rear of the column. The company (if it be a company) must therefore be countermarched, if necessary. When the rear guard halts, the skirmishers must always face to the side of the enemy. In retiring they must constantly look behind and on the flanks to avoid surprise, and to rally if required. They must seize the positions of strength that the route may offer, to delay and oppose the enemy, falling back from one position to another.

In passing a bridge, ford, or defile, the reserve will pass first, and extend along the farther side, facing the enemy, to cover the passage of the skirmishers. The skirmishers on approaching the bridge-head will make a stand, the flanks will immediately commence the passage, the extreme right and left files firing and at once retreating, the other files following these in succession, the centre files following last of all. The old line of skirmishers form for a reserve, two hundred paces beyond the bridge, and the late reserve, now deployed, take their places.

The duty of skirmishing in the rear guard is so exhausting, that frequent reliefs are absolutely necessary.

# MILITARY AND NAVAL PUBLICATIONS

FROM THE PRESS OF

## D. VAN NOSTRAND,

192 BROADWAY,

NEW YORK.

---

A large Stock of English, French, and American Military Works, constantly on hand.

Copies of any of these Books sent free by mail on rece_ _ of the Catalogue price.

192 Broadway, New York.

# Military and Naval Publications

*FROM THE PRESS OF*

## D. VAN NOSTRAND.

*Copies of any of the books on this Catalogue sent* FREE *by mail, on receipt of the price.*

### SCOTT'S MILITARY DICTIONARY.

Comprising Technical Definitions; Information on Raising and Keeping Troops; Actual Service, including makeshifts and improved *materiel*, and Law, Government, Regulation, and Administration relating to Land Forces. By Colonel H. L. Scott, Inspector-General U. S. A. 1 vol., large 8vo, fully illustrated, half morocco. $5.

"We cannot speak too much in legitimate praise of this work."—*National Intelligencer.*

"We cordially commend it to public favor."—*Washington Globe.*

"This comprehensive and skilfully prepared work, supplies a want that has long been felt, and will be peculiarly valuable at this time as a book of reference."—*Boston Commercial Bulletin.*

"The Military Dictionary is splendidly got up in every way, and reflects credit on the publisher. The officers of every company in the service should possess it."—*N. Y. Tablet.*

"The work is more properly a Military Encyclopædia, and is profusely illustrated with engravings. It appears to contain every thing that can be wanted in the shape of information by officers of all grades."—*Philadelphia North American.*

"This book is really an Encyclopædia, both elementary and technical, and as such occupies a gap in military literature which has long been most inconveniently vacant. This book meets a present popular want, and will be secured not only by those embarking in the profession, but by a great number of civilians, who are determined to follow the descriptions, and to understand the philosophy of the various movements of the campaign. Indeed, no tolerably good library would be complete without the work."—*N. Y. Times.*

## Rifles and Rifle Practice.

An Elementary Treatise on the Theory of Rifle Firing; explaining the causes of Inaccuracy of Firing, and the manner of correcting it; with descriptions of the Infantry Rifles of Europe and the United States, their Balls and Cartridges. By Capt. C. M. WILCOX, U. S. A. New edition, with engravings and cuts. Green cloth. $1 75.

ADJUTANT-GENERAL'S OFFICE, }
Washington, June 28th, 1859. }

SIR:—I am instructed to inform you that the War Department will take one thousand copies of Wilcox's Treatise on "Rifles and Rifle Practice," now being published by you.

I am, sir, very respectfully, your obedient servant,
E. D. TOWNSEND,
*Assistant Adjutant-General.*

D. VAN NOSTRAND, Esq.,
Publisher, city of New York.

"The book will be found intensely interesting to all who are watching the changes in the art of war arising from the introduction of the new rifled arms. We recommend to our readers to buy the book."—*Military Gazette.*

"This book is quite original in its character. That character is completeness. It renders a study of most of the works on the rifle that have been published quite unnecessary. We cordially recommend the book."—*United Service Gazette, London.*

## SCHOOL OF THE GUIDES.

Designed for the use of the Militia of the United States. Flexible cloth. 50 cents.

"The work is carefully got up, and is illustrated by numerous figures, which make the positions of the guides plain to the commonest understanding. Those of our sergeants who wish to be 'posted' in their duties should procure a copy."—*Sunday Mercury, Philadelphia.*

"It has received high praise, and will prove of great service in perfecting the drill of our Militia."—*N. American and U. S. Gazette, Philadelphia.*

"This neat hand-book of the elementary movements on which the art of the tactician is based, reflects great credit on Col. Le Gal, whose reputation is deservedly high among military men. No soldier should be without the 'School of the Guides.'"—*N. Y. Daily News.*

## Army Officer's Pocket Companion.

Principally designed for Staff Officers in the Field. Partly translated from the French of M. DE ROUVRE, Lieutenant-Colonel of the French Staff Corps, with additions from Standard American, French, and English Authorities. By WM P. CRAIGHILL, First Lieutenant U. S. Corps of Engineers, Assistant Professor of Engineering at the U. S. Military Academy, West Point. 1 vol. 18mo. Full roan. $1 50.

"I have carefully examined Capt. CRAIGHILL's Pocket Companion. I find it one of the very best works of the kind I have ever seen. Any Army or Volunteer Officer who will make himself acquainted with the contents of this little book, will seldom be ignorant of his duties in camp or field."
H. W. HALLECK,
*Major-General U. S. A.*

"I have carefully examined the 'Manual for Staff Officers in the Field.' It is a most invaluable work, admirable in arrangement, perspicuously written, abounding in most useful matters, and such a book as should be the constant pocket companion of every army officer, Regular and Volunteer."
G. W. CULLUM,
*Brigadier-General U. S. A.,*
*Chief of General Halleck's Staff.*

---

## Halleck's International Law.

International Law; or, Rules Regulating the Intercourse of States in Peace and War. By Major-Gen. H. W. HALLECK, Commanding the Army. 1 vol. 8vo, law sheep. $6.

---

### DICTIONARY OF ALL OFFICERS IN THE UNITED STATES ARMY,

From 1789 to January 1st, 1853, and of the Navy and Marine Corps. Second edition, with a Supplement, bringing it down to January 1, 1860. By Col. CHAS. K. GARDNER. 1 vol. 12mo, cloth. $3.

[*By authority.*]

## CASEY'S
# NEW INFANTRY TACTICS,

For the Instruction, Exercise, and Manœuvres of the Soldier, a Company, Line of Skirmishers, Battalion, Brigade, or Corps d'Armée. By Brig.-Gen. SILAS CASEY, U. S. A. 3 vols. 24mo. Lithographed plates. $2 50.

Vol. I.—School of the Soldier; School of the Company; Instruction for Skirmishers.

Vol. II.—School of the Battalion.

Vol. III.—Evolutions of a Brigade; Evolutions of a Corps d'Armée.

WAR DEPARTMENT, Washington, August 11, 1862.

The System of Infantry Tactics prepared by Brig.-Gen. Silas Casey, U. S. A., having been approved by the President, is adopted for the instruction of the Infantry of the Armies of the United States, whether Regular, Volunteer, or Militia, with the following modifications, viz.:

*First*, That portion which requires that two companies shall be permanently detached from the battalion as skirmishers, will be suspended.

*Second*, In Title First, Article First, the following will be substituted for Paragraph 6. viz.:

"A regiment is composed of ten companies, which will be habitually posted from right to left in the following order; first, sixth, fourth, ninth, third, eighth, fifth, tenth, seventh, second, according to the rank of Captain."      EDWIN M. STANTON,
*Secretary of War.*

---

A
# Treatise on the Camp and March.

With which is connected the Construction of Field Works and Military Bridges; with an Appendix of Artillery Ranges, &c. For the use of Volunteers and Militia in the United States. By Captain HENRY D. GRAFTON, U. S. A. 1 vol. 12mo, cloth. 75 cents.

## LIEBER ON GUERILLA PARTIES.

Guerilla Parties considered with reference to the Laws and Usages of War. Written at the request of Major-Gen. Henry W. Halleck, General-in-Chief of the Army of the United States. By FRANCIS LIEBER. 12mo, paper. 25 cents.

HEADQUARTERS OF THE ARMY,
Washington, Aug. 6, 1862.

DR. FRANCIS LIEBER:

My Dear Doctor—Having heard that you have given much attention to the usages and customs of war as practised in the present age, and especially to the matter of guerilla war, I hope you may find it convenient to give to the public your views on that subject. The rebel authorities claim the right to send men, in the garb of peaceful citizens, to waylay and attack our troops, to burn bridges and houses, and to destroy property and persons within our lines. They demand that such persons be treated as ordinary belligerents, and that when captured they have extended to them the same rights as other prisoners of war. They also threaten that if such persons be punished as marauders and spies, they will retaliate by executing our prisoners of war in their possession.

I particularly request your views on these questions.

Very respectfully, your obedient servant,

H. W. HALLECK, *General-in-Chief U. S. A.*

---

## HAND-BOOK OF ARTILLERY,

For the Service of the United States Army and Militia. New and revised edition. By Major JOSEPH ROBERTS, U. S. A. 1 vol. 18mo, cloth. $1 25.

The following is an extract from a Report made by the committee appointed at a meeting of the staff of the Artillery School at Fort Monroe, Va., to whom the commanding officer of the school had referred this work:

\* \* \* "In the opinion of your Committee, the arrangement of the subjects and the selection of the several questions and answers have been judicious. The work is one which may be advantageously used for reference by the officers, and is admirably adapted to the instruction of non-commissioned officers and privates of Artillery.

"Your Committee do, therefore, recommend that it be substituted as a text-book in place of 'Burns' Questions and Answers on Artillery.'"

(Signed,) I. VOGDES, *Capt. 1st Artillery.*
(Signed,) E. O. C. ORD, *Capt. 3d Artillery.*
(Signed,) J. A. HASKIN, *Bvt. Maj. and Capt. 1st Artillery.*

## The Political and Military History
### OF THE
# CAMPAIGN OF WATERLOO.

Translated from the French of General BARON DE JOMINI. By Capt. S. V. BENÉT, U. S. Ordnance. 1 vol. 12mo, cloth, second edition. 75 cents.

"Baron Jomini has the reputation of being one of the greatest military historians and critics of the century. His merits have been recognized by the highest military authorities in Europe, and were rewarded in a conspicuous manner by the greatest military power in Christendom. He learned the art of war in the school of experience, the best and only finishing school of the soldier. He served with distinction in nearly all the campaigns of Napoleon, and it was mainly from the gigantic military operations of this matchless master of the art that he was enabled to discover its true principles, and to ascertain the best means of their application in the infinity of combinations which actual war presents. Jomini criticizes the details of Waterloo with great science, and yet in a manner that interests the general reader as well as the professional."—*New York World.*

"The present volume is the concluding portion of his great work, 'Vie Politique et Militaire de Napoléon,' published in 1826. Capt. Benét's translation of it has been for some time before the public, and has now reached a second edition; it is very ably executed, and forms a work which will always be interesting, and especially so at a time when military affairs are uppermost in the public mind."—*Philadelphia North American.*

## *Maxims and Instructions on the Art of War.*

Maxims, Advice, and Instructions on the Art of War; or, A Practical Military Guide for the use of Soldiers of all Arms and of all Countries. Translated from the French by Captain LENDY, Director of the Practical Military College, late of the French Staff, &c., &c. 1 vol. 18mo, cloth. 75 cents.

"A book of maxims, that is not as dry as a cask of 'remainder biscuit,' is a novelty in literature. The little volume before us is an exception to the general rule. It presents the suggestion of common sense in military affairs, with a certain brilliancy and point. One may read it purely or entertainment, and not be disappointed. At the same time, it is full of practical instructions of great value. When found in the pocket of an officer of volunteers, it will be the right book in the right place."—*N. Y. Tribune.*

## Nolan's System for Training Cavalry Horses.

By KENNER GARRARD, Captain Fifth Cavalry, U. S. A. 1 vol. 12mo, cloth. Twenty-four lithographed plates. $1 50.

\* \* \* "We are glad when competent men bring forward works that are intended to facilitate the formation of an effective cavalry force. Of this class is 'Nolan's System for Training Cavalry Horses,' prepared for use in this country, by Captain Kenner Garrard, U. S. A. Captain Noan was distinguished in the British service for his knowledge of the cavalry arm, and for his general talents. As the work had become out of print, Captain Garrard has done well in reproducing it; he has added to it a chapter on Rarey's Method of Training Horses, and another on Horse Shoeing. The volume is well illustrated. It cannot be too warmly commended to general use."—*Boston Daily Evening Traveller.*

"It explains a perfectly successful method of gaining the mastery over the most refractory horse, and is no less adapted for the use of the rider for exercise, business, or pleasure, than of the cavalry officer. By the plan of the author, the time of training is greatly shortened; the progress is so gradual that it never makes the horse namiable, and the successive lessons tend to the development of mutual love and admiration between the parties."—*N. Y. Tribune.*

## Monroe's Company Drill.

The Company Drill of the Infantry of the Line, together with the Skirmishing Drill of the Company and Battalion, after the method of Gen. LE LOUTEREL. And Bayonet Fencing. By Col. J. MONROE, 22d Regt. N. Y. S. M. 24mo, cloth. 50 cents.

## CAVALRY:
### ITS HISTORY, MANAGEMENT, AND USES IN WAR.

By J. ROEMER, late an Officer of Cavalry in the service of the Netherlands. 1 vol. 8vo. With over two hundred beautifully engraved illustrations. $5 00.

# THE ARTILLERIST'S MANUAL.

Compiled from various sources, and adapted to the service of the United States. Profusely illustrated with woodcuts and engravings on stone. Second edition, revised and corrected, with valuable additions. By Gen. JOHN GIBBON, U. S. A. 1 vol. 8vo, half roan, $5; half russia, $6.

---

## AMERICAN MILITARY BRIDGES,

With India-Rubber and Galvanized Iron Pontons and Trestle Supporters, prepared for the use of the Armies of the United States. By Brig.-Gen. GEO. W. CULLUM, Major Corps of Engineers, U. S. A., Chief of the Staff of Major-Gen. Halleck. Second edition, with notes and two additional chapters. 1 vol. 8vo, with plates. *In press.*

---

## *New Bayonet Exercise.*

A New Manual of the Bayonet, for the Army and Militia of the United States. By Colonel J. C. KELTON, U. S. A. With thirty beautifully-engraved plates. Red cloth. $1 75.

This Manual was prepared for the use of the Corps of Cadets, and has been introduced at the Military Academy with satisfactory results. It is simply the theory of the attack and defence of the sword applied to the bayonet, on the authority of men skilled in the use of arms.

The Manual contains practical lessons in Fencing, and prescribes the defence against Cavalry, and the manner of conducting a contest with a Swordsman.

"This work merits a favorable reception at the hands of all military men. It contains all the instruction necessary to enable an officer to drill his men in the use of this weapon. The introduction of the sabre bayonet in our army, renders a knowledge of the exercise more imperative."—*N. Y. Times.*

# THE "C. S. A."
### AND THE
## BATTLE OF BULL RUN.

(A Letter to an English Friend.) By J. G. BARNARD, Major of Engineers, U. S. A., Brigadier-General, and Chief Engineer, Army of the Potomac. With five maps. 1 vol. 8vo, cloth. $1 50.

"This book was begun by the author as a letter to a friend in England, but as he proceeded and his MSS. increased in magnitude, he changed his original plan, and the book is the result. General Barnard gives by far the best, most comprehensible and complete account of the Battle of Bull Run we have seen. It is illustrated by some beautifully drawn maps, prepared for the War Department by the topographical engineers. He demonstrates to a certainty that but for the causeless panic the day might not have been lost. The author writes with vigor and earnestness, and has contributed one of the most valuable records yet published of the history of the war."—*Boston Commercial Bulletin.*

"A spirited and reliable view of the true character of the secession movement, and a correct account of the Battle of Bull Run, by a military man whose qualifications for the task are equalled but by few persons."—*Cincinnati Gazette.*

"The work is clearly written, and can but leave the impression upon every reader's mind that it is truth. We commend it to the perusal of every one who wants an intelligent, truthful, and graphic description of the 'C. S. A.' and the Battle of Bull Run."—*New York Observer.*

## Rhymed Tactics, by "Gov."

1 vol. 18mo, paper. With portraits. 25 cents.

"It will strike the military man, familiar with the tedious routine of drill, by theory, practice and memory, as a most unique and valuable method of strengthening the latter, with the least mental exertion. The author is a thorough soldier, and his ability as a rhymester will be conceded by any intelligent reader."—*N. Y. Leader.*

"Our author deserves great credit for the ingenuity he has displayed in putting into verse a manual which would at first glance seem to defy the most persistent efforts of the rhymer. The book contains a number of illustrations, representing some of the more difficult positions, in the figures of which, portraits of several prominent officers of the New York Volunteers may be recognized."—*N. Y. Times.*

## Siege of Bomarsund (1854).

Journals of Operations of the Artillery and Engineers. Published by permission of the Minister of War. Illustrated by maps and plans. Translated from the French by an Army Officer. 1 vol. 12mo, cloth. 75 cents.

---

## European Ordnance and Iron-Clad Defenses,

With some account of the American Practice, embracing the Fabrication and Test of Heavy Guns; Projectiles and Rifling; the Manufacture and Test of Armor, from official data, with a detailed account of English experiments; the principles, structure, and classification of Iron-Clad Vessels; Marine Steam Machinery, &c. By ALEX. L. HOLLEY, B. P., author of "American and European Railway Practice," &c. 1 vol. 8vo, cloth. With 250 illustrations. *In press.*

---

### HOLLEY'S RAILWAY PRACTICE.

American and European Railway Practice, in the Economical Generation of Steam, including the materials and construction of Coal-burning Boilers, Combustion, the Variable Blast, Vaporization, Circulation, Superheating, Supplying and Heating Feed-water, &c., and the adaptation of Wood and Coke-burning Engines to Coal-burning; and in Permanent Way, including Road-bed, Sleepers, Rails, Joint Fastenings, Street Railways, &c., &c. By ALEXANDER L. HOLLEY, B. P. With 77 lithographed plates. 1 vol. folio, cloth. $10.

## ELEMENTS OF
## Military Art and History.

Comprising the History of the Tactics of the separate Arms, the Combination of the Arms, and the minor operations of war. By EDWARD DE LA BARRE DUPARCQ, Captain of Engineers, and Professor of the Military Art in the Imperial School of Saint Cyr. Translated by Brig.-Gen. GEORGE W. CULLUM, U. S. A., Chief of the Staff of Major-General H. W. Halleck, U. S. A. 1 vol. 8vo, cloth. $4.

---

## BENÉT'S MILITARY LAW.

A Treatise on Military Law and the Practice of Courts-Martial. By Capt. S. V. BENÉT, Ordnance Department, U. S. A., late Assistant Professor of Ethics, Law, &c., Military Academy, West Point. Adopted as the Text-Book at the Military Academy, West Point. 1 vol. 8vo, law sheep. $3.

JUDGE ADVOCATE GENERAL'S OFFICE,
October 13, 1862.

\* \* \* So far as I have been enabled to examine this volume, it seems to me carefully and accurately prepared, and I am satisfied that you have rendered an acceptable service to the army and the country by its publication at this moment. In consequence of the gigantic proportions so suddenly assumed by the military operations of the Government, there have been necessarily called into the field, from civil life, a vast number of officers, unacquainted from their previous studies and pursuits, both with the principles of military law and with the course of judicial proceedings under it. To all such, this treatise will prove an easily accessible storehouse of knowledge, which it is equally the duty of the soldier in command to acquire, as it is to learn to draw his sword against the common enemy. The military spirit of our people now being thoroughly aroused, added to a growing conviction that in future we may have to depend quite as much upon the bayonet as upon the ballot box for the preservation of our institutions, cannot fail to secure to this work an extended and earnest appreciation. In bringing the results of legislation and of decisions upon the questions down to so recent a period, the author has added greatly to the interest and usefulness of the volume. Very respectfully, your obedient servant,
J. HOLT.

## TEXAS,
### AND ITS LATE MILITARY OCCUPATION AND EVACUATION.

By Capt. EDWIN D. PHILLIPS, 1st Infantry, U. S. A. 8vo, paper. 25 cents.

---

### OFFICIAL ARMY REGISTER FOR 1862.

New edition. 8vo, paper. 50 cents.

---

### *Nautical Routine and Stowage.*

With Short Rules in Navigation. By JOHN MCLEOD MURPHY and WM. N. JEFFERS, Jr., U. S. N. 1 vol. 8vo, cloth. $2 50.

---

### Mordecai's Report.

Military Commission to Europe in 1855 and 1856. Report of Major ALFRED MORDECAI, U. S. Ordnance Department. 1 vol. folio. With views and maps. $2 50.

---

### Delafield's Report.

Report on the Art of War in Europe in 1854, 1855, and 1856. By Col. R. DELAFIELD, Corps of Engineers, U. S. A. 1 vol. folio, cloth. With maps and views. $5.

---

### HINTS TO COMPANY OFFICERS.

By Capt. C. C. ANDREWS, 3d Regt. Minnesota Vols. 1 vol. 18mo, cloth. 50 cents.

# VIELE'S HAND-BOOK.

Hand-Book for Active Service, containing Practical Instructions in Campaign Duties. For the use of Volunteers. By Brig.-Gen. EGBERT L. VIELE, U. S. A. 12mo, cloth. $1.

## Gunnery in 1858.

A Treatise on Rifles, Cannon, and Sporting Arms. By WM. GREENER, C. E. 1 vol. 8vo, cloth. $3.

## Manual of Heavy Artillery.

For the use of Volunteers. 1 vol. 12mo, red cloth. 75 cents.

"Should be in the hands of every Artillerist."—*N. Y. Illustrated News.*

"This is a concise and well-prepared Manual, adapted to the wants of Volunteers. The instruction, which is of an important nature, is presented in a simple and clear style, such as will be easily understood. The volume is also illustrated with explanatory cuts and drawings. It is a work of practical value, and one needed at the present time in the service."—*Boston Commercial Bulletin.*

"An indispensable Manual for all who wish easily and accurately to learn the school of the Artillerist."—*N. Y. Commercial Advertiser.*

## AUSTRIAN INFANTRY TACTICS.

Evolutions of the Line as practised by the Austrian Infantry, and adopted in 1853. Translated by Capt. C. M. WILCOX, Seventh Regiment U. S. Infantry. 1 vol. 12mo. Three large plates. Cloth. $1.

## NEW MANUAL OF SWORD AND SABRE EXERCISE.

By Colonel J. C. KELTON, U. S. A. Thirty plates. *In press.*

## Benton's Ordnance and Gunnery.

A Course of Instruction in Ordnance and Gunnery, compiled for the use of the Cadets of the United States Military Academy. By Capt. J. G. BENTON, Ordnance Department, late Instructor of Ordnance and Gunnery, Military Academy, West Point. Principal Assistant to Chief of Ordnance, U. S. A. Second edition, revised and enlarged. 1 vol. 8vo, half morocco, cuts. $4.

"We cannot commend this work too highly, both for the substance it contains, and the highly finished manner in which it has been issued by the publisher. There is no one book within the range of our military reading and study, that contains more to recommend it upon the subject of which it treats. It is as full and complete as the narrow compass of a single volume would admit, and the reputation of the author as a scientific and practical artillerist, is a sufficient guarantee for the correctness of his statements and deductions, and the thoroughness of his labors."—*N. Y. Observer.*

"A GREAT MILITARY WORK.—We have before us a bound volume of nearly 600 pages, which is a complete and exhaustive 'Course of Instruction in Ordnance and Gunnery,' as its title states, and goes into every department of the science, including gunpowder, projectiles, cannon, carriages, machines and implements, small arms, pyrotechny, science of gunnery, loading, pointing and discharging firearms, different kinds of fires, effects of projectiles and employment of artillery. These severally form chapter heads, and give thorough information on the subjects on which they treat. The most valuable and interesting information on all the above topics, including the history, manufacture, and use of small arms, is here concentrated in compact and convenient form, making a work of rare merit and standard excellence. The work is abundantly and clearly illustrated."—*Boston Traveller.*

---

### SIEGE AND REDUCTION OF
# Fort Pulaski, Georgia.

Papers on Practical Engineering. No. 8. Official Report to the U. S. Engineer Department of the Siege and Reduction of Fort Pulaski, Ga., February, March, and April, 1862. By Brig.-General Q. A. GILLMORE, U. S. A. Illustrated by Maps and Views. 1 vol. 8vo, cloth. $2 50.

# SWORD-PLAY.
## THE MILITIAMAN'S MANUAL AND SWORD-PLAY WITHOUT A MASTER.

Rapier and Broad-Sword Exercises copiously Explained and Illustrated; Small-Arm Light Infantry Drill of the United States Army; Infantry Manual of Percussion Muskets; Company Drill of the United States Cavalry. By Major M. W. BERRIMAN, engaged for the last thirty years in the practical instruction of Military Students. Second edition. 1 vol. 12mo, red cloth. $1.

"Captain Berriman has had thirty years' experience in teaching military students, and his work is written in a simple, clear, and soldierly style. It is illustrated with twelve plates, and is one of the cheapest and most complete works of the kind published in this country."—*N. Y. World.*

"This work will be found very valuable to all persons seeking military instruction; but it recommends itself most especially to officers, and those who have to use the sword or sabre. We believe it is the only work on the use of the sword published in this country."—*N. Y. Tablet.*

## *Manual for Engineer Troops.*

Consisting of—
    Part I. Ponton Drill.
        II. Practical Operations of a Siege.
        III. School of the Sap.
        IV. Military Mining.
        V. Construction of Batteries.

By Captain J. C. DUANE, Corps of Engineers, U. S. A. 1 vol. 12mo, half morocco, with plates. $2.

"I have carefully examined Capt. J. C. Duane's 'Manual for Engineer Troops,' and do not hesitate to pronounce it the very best work on the subject of which it treats."
        H. W. HALLECK, *Major-General, U. S. A.*

"A work of this kind has been much needed in our military literature. For the army's sake, I hope the book will have a wide circulation among its officers."
        G. B. McCLELLAN, *Major-General, U. S. A.*

# Gunnery Instructions.

Simplified for the Volunteer Officers of the U. S. Navy, with hints to Executive and other Officers. By Lieut.-Commander EDWARD BARRETT, U. S. N., Instructor in Gunnery, Navy Yard, Brooklyn. Second edition, revised and enlarged. 1 vol. 12mo, cloth. $1 25.

"It is a thorough work, treating plainly on its subject, and contains also some valuable hints to executive officers. No officer in the volunteer navy should be without a copy."—*Boston Evening Traveller.*

"This work, which is appropriately dedicated to the Acting Masters and Masters' Mates of the United States Navy, contains detailed and specific instructions on all points connected with the use and management of guns of every kind in the naval service. It has full illustrations, and many of these of the most elementary character, especially designed for the use of volunteers in the navy. The duties of executive officers and of the division officers are so clearly set forth, that 'he who runs may read' and understand. The manual exercise is explicit, and rendered simple by diagrams. Forms of watch and quarter bills are given; and at the close there is a table of ranges according to the kind and caliber of gun, the weight of the ball and the charge of powder. A valuable little hand-book."—*Philadelphia Inquirer.*

"I have looked through Lieut. Barrett's book, and think it will be very valuable to the volunteer officers who are now in the naval service." C. R. P. RODGERS,
*Commanding U. S. Steam Frigate Wabash.*

---

## ELEMENTARY INSTRUCTION IN NAVAL ORDNANCE AND GUNNERY.

By JAMES H. WARD, Commander U. S. N., Author of "Naval Tactics," and "Steam for the Million." New edition, revised and enlarged. 8vo, cloth. $2.

"It conveys an amount of information in the same space to be found nowhere else, and given with a clearness which renders it useful as well to the general as the professional inquirer."—*N. Y. Evening Post.*

"This volume is a standard treatise upon the subject to which it is devoted. It abounds in valuable information upon all the points bearing upon Naval Gunnery."—*N. Y. Commercial Advertiser.*

"The work is an exceedingly valuable one, and is opportunely issued."—*Boston Journal.*

Notes on Screw Propulsion, its Rise and History. By Capt. W. H. WALKER, U. S. N. 1 vol. 8vo, cloth. 75 cents.

\* \* \* "After thoroughly demonstrating the efficiency of the screw, Mr. Walker proceeds to point out the various other points to be attended to in order to secure an efficient man-of-war, and eulogizes throughout the readiness of the British Admiralty to test every novelty calculated to give satisfactory results. \* \* \* Commander Walker's book contains an immense amount of concise, practical data, and every item of information recorded, fully proves that the various points bearing upon it have been well considered previously to expressing an opinion."—*London Mining Journal.*

"Every engineer should have it in his library."—*American Engineer.*

## *A Treatise on Ordnance and Naval Gunnery.*

Compiled and arranged as a Text-Book for the U. S. Naval Academy. By Lieut.-Commander EDWARD SIMPSON, U. S. N. Second edition, revised and enlarged. 1 vol. 8vo, plates and cuts, half morocco. $4.

BUREAU OF ORDNANCE AND HYDROGRAPHY, July 9th, 1859.

Sir:—\* \* \* The Secretary of the Navy approves of the use of this work as a text-book for the Academy. \* \* \*
Respectfully, your obedient servant,
D. N. INGRAHAM, *Chief of Bureau.*
Capt. G. S. BLAKE,
Superintendent of Naval Academy, Annapolis, Md.

"It is scarcely necessary for us to say that a work prepared by a writer so practically conversant with all the subjects of which he treats, and who has such a reputation for scientific ability, cannot fail to take at once a high place among the text-books of our naval service. It has been approved by the Secretary of the Navy, and will henceforth be one of the standard authorities on all matters connected with Naval Gunnery."—*N. Y. Herald.*

"Originally designed as a text-book, it is now enlarged, and so far modified in its plan as to make it an invaluable hand-book for the naval officer. It is comprehensive—preserving the cream of many of the best books on ordnance and naval gunnery, and is printed and illustrated in the most admirable manner."—*N. Y. World.*

## Notes on Sea-Coast Defence,

Consisting of Sea-Coast Fortification; the Fifteen-Inch Gun, and Casemate Embrasures. By Gen. J. G. BARNARD, Corps of Engineers, U. S. A. 1 vol. 8vo, cloth, plates. $1 50.

"This small volume, by one of the most accomplished officers in the United States service, is especially valuable at this time. Concisely and thoroughly Major Barnard discusses the subjects included in this volume, and gives information that will be read with great profit by military men, and by all interested in the art of war as a defensive force."—*N. Y. Commercial.*

"It is no light compliment when we say that Major Barnard's book does no discredit to the corps to which he belongs. He writes concisely, and with a thorough knowledge of his subject."—*Russell's Army and Navy Gazette.*

## STEAM FOR THE MILLION.

A Popular Treatise on Steam and its Application to the Useful Arts, especially to Navigation. By J. H. WARD, Commander, U. S. N. New and revised edition. 1 vol. 8vo, cloth. $1.

"A most excellent work for the young engineer and general reader. Many facts relating to the management of the boiler and engine are set forth with a simplicity of language, and perfection of detail, that brings the subject home to the reader. Mr. Ward is also peculiarly happy in his illustrations."—*American Engineer.*

## STANDING ORDERS OF THE SEVENTH REGIMENT, NATIONAL GUARD.

For the Regulation and Government of the Regiment in the Field or in Quarters. By A. DURYEE, Colonel. New edition. Flexible cloth. 40 cents.

"This, which is a new edition of a popular work, cannot fail to be eagerly sought after, as presenting clearly and succinctly the principles of organization and discipline of a most favorite corps. An appropriate index facilitates reference to the matter of the volume."—*New Yorker.*

# HISTORY

## OF THE

## United States Naval Academy,

With Biographical Sketches, and the names of all the Superintendents, Professors, and Graduates, to which is added a Record of some of the earliest Votes by Congress, of Thanks, Medals, and Swords to Naval Officers. By EDWARD CHAUNCEY MARSHALL, A. M. 1 vol. 12mo, cloth, plates. $1.

"The book before us affords a good account of the naval school from its first establishment under the auspices of Secretary Bancroft, with full statements of the regulations, requisites for admission, course of study, etc. It is a seasonable and useful contribution to the history of education in this country."—*N. Y. Independent.*

"This is a most welcome volume. All that throws light on the history of our army and navy, now needs study; and the Naval Academy, though really so recent, well deserves a history. Mr. Marshall has depicted, in clear and graphic language, the vain struggle for years to give our navy, what the navy of every nation has, an academy to form the young officers for their important duties."—*N. Y. Historical Magazine.*

"Every naval man will find it not only a pleasant companion, but an invaluable book of reference. It is seldom that so much information is made accessible in so agreeable a manner in so small a space."—*N. Y. Times.*

## TOTTEN'S NAVAL TEXT-BOOK.

Naval Text-Book and Dictionary, compiled for the use of the Midshipmen of the U. S. Navy. By Commander B. J. TOTTEN, U. S. N. Second and revised edition. 1 vol. 12mo. $2 50.

"This work is prepared for the Midshipmen of the United States Navy. It is a complete manual of instructions as to the duties which pertain to their office, and appears to have been prepared with great care, avoiding errors and inaccuracies which had crept into a former edition of the work, and embracing valuable additional matter. It is a book which should be in the hands of every midshipman, and officers of high rank in the navy would often find it a useful companion."—*Boston Journal.*

THE
# AUTOMATON REGIMENT,
### OR
### Infantry Soldiers' Practical Instructor.

For all REGIMENTAL MOVEMENTS IN THE FIELD. By G. DOUGLAS BREWERTON, U. S. Army. Neatly put up in boxes, price $1; when sent by mail, $1 40.

The "Automaton Regiment" is a simple combination of blocks and counters, so arranged and designated by a carefully considered contrast of colors, that it supplies the student with a perfect miniature regiment, in which the position in the battalion of each company, and of every officer and man in each division, company, platoon and section, is clearly indicated. It supplies the studious soldier with the means whereby he can consult his "tactics," and at the same time join practice to theory by manœuvring a mimic regiment.

HEADQUARTERS, MILITARY GOVERNOR,
Department of the South,
Beaufort, South Carolina, Oct. 21st, 1862.

I hereby certify that I have examined the "Automaton Regiment," invented by G. Douglas Brewerton, late of the U. S. Regular Army, and now serving as a Volunteer Aid upon my military staff, and believe that his invention will prove a useful and valuable assistant to every student of military tactics. I take pleasure in recommending it accordingly.
R. SAXTON,
*Brig.-General Volunteers.*

---

# A System of Target Practice.

For the use of Troops when armed with the Musket, Rifle-Musket, Rifle, or Carbine. Prepared, principally from the French, by Captain HENRY HETH, 10th Infantry, U. S. A. 50 cents.

## THE
# AUTOMATON COMPANY;
### OR,
### Infantry Soldiers' Practical Instructor.

For all COMPANY MOVEMENTS IN THE FIELD. By G. Douglas Brewerton, U. S. A. Price in boxes, $1 25; when sent by mail, $1 95.

---

## THE
# AUTOMATON BATTERY;
### OR,
### Artillerists' Practical Instructor.

For all MOUNTED ARTILLERY MANŒUVRES IN THE FIELD. By G. Douglas Brewerton, U. S. A. Price in boxes, $1; when sent by mail, $1 40.

---

## UNION FOUNDATIONS.

A Study of American Nationality, as a Fact of Science. By Capt. E. B. Hunt, Corps of Engineers, U. S. A. 1 vol., 8vo., cloth.

---

## MODELS OF FORTIFICATIONS.

### VAUBAN'S FIRST SYSTEM.
One Front and two Bastions—Scale, 20 yards to an inch.

### THE MODERN SYSTEM.
One Front—Scale, 20 yards to an inch.

### FIELD-WORKS.
The Square Redoubt—Scale, 5 yards to an inch.

Mr. Kimber's three volumes, viz., Vauban's First System, The Modern System, and Field-Works, will accompany the models.

## *Lessons and Practical Notes on Steam,*

The Steam Engine, Propellers, &c., &c., for Young Marine Engineers, Students, and others. By the late W. R. KING, U. S. N. Revised by Chief-Engineer J. W. KING, U. S. N. Third edition, enlarged. 8vo, cloth. $1 50.

"This is a new edition of a valuable work of the late W. R. King, U. S. N. It contains lessons and practical notes on Steam and the Steam Engine, Propellers, &c. It is calculated to be of great use to young marine engineers, students, and others. The text is illustrated and explained by numerous diagrams and representations of machinery. This new edition has been revised and enlarged by Chief Engineer J. W. King, U. S. N., brother to the deceased author of the work."—*Boston Daily Advertiser.*

"This is one of the best, because eminently plain and practical, treatises on the Steam Engine ever published."—*Philadelphia Press.*

"Its re-publication at this time, when so many young men are entering the service as naval engineers, is most opportune. Each of them ought to have a copy."—*Philadelphia Evening Bulletin.*

## MANUAL OF INTERNAL RULES AND REGULATIONS FOR MEN-OF-WAR.

By Commodore U. P. LEVY, U. S. N., late Flag-Officer commanding U. S. Naval Force in the Mediterranean, &c. Third edition, revised and enlarged. With Rules and Regulations for the Engineer Department. By A. C. STIMERS, Chief-Engineer U. S. N. Flexible blue cloth. 50 cents.

"Among the professional publications for which we are indebted to the war, we willingly give a prominent place to this useful little Manual of Rules and Regulations to be observed on board of ships of war. Its authorship is a sufficient guarantee for its accuracy and practical value; and as a guide to young officers in providing for the discipline, police, and sanitary government of the vessels under their command, we know of nothing superior."—*N. Y. Herald.*

"Should be in the hands of every naval officer, of whatever grade, and will not come amiss to any intelligent mariner."—*Boston Traveller.*

# NAVAL LIGHT ARTILLERY.

Instruction for Naval Light Artillery, afloat and ashore, prepared and arranged for the U. S. Naval Academy. By Lieut. W. H. PARKER, U. S. N. Second edition revised by Lieut. S. B. LUCE, U. S. N., Assistant Instructor of Gunnery and Tactics at the United State. Naval Academy. 1 vol. 8vo, cloth, with 22 plates. $1 50.

"The service for which this is the text-book of instruction, is of special importance in the present war. The use of light boat-pieces is constant and important, and young officers are frequently obliged to leave their boats, take their pieces ashore, and manœuvre them as field artillery. Not unfrequently, also, they are incorporated, when ashore, with troops, and must handle their guns like the artillery soldiers of a battery. 'The Exercise of the Howitzer Afloat' was prepared and arranged by Captain Dahlgren, whose name gives additional sanction and value to the book. A Manual for the Sword and Pistol is also given. The plates are numerous and exceedingly clear, and the whole typography excellent."—*Philadelphia Inquirer.*

## EVOLUTIONS OF FIELD BATTERIES OF ARTILLERY.

Translated from the French, and arranged for the Army and Militia of the United States. By Gen. ROBERT ANDERSON, U. S. A. Published by order of the War Department. 1 vol. cloth, 32 plates. $1.

WAR DEPARTMENT, Nov. 2d, 1859.

The System of "Evolutions of Field Batteries," translated from the French, and arranged for the service of the United States, by Major Robert Anderson, of the 1st Regiment of Artillery, having been approved by the President, is published for the information and government of the army.

All Evolutions of Field Batteries not embraced in this system, are prohibited, and those herein prescribed will be strictly observed.

J. B. FLOYD, *Secretary of War.*

"This system having been adopted by the War Department, is to the artillerist what Hardee's Tactics is to the infantry soldier; the want of a work like this has been seriously felt, and will be

www.ingramcontent.com/pod-product-compliance
Lightning Source LLC
Chambersburg PA
CBHW020252170426
43202CB00008B/333